A RICHER VISION

'Communication and Development' Series

A RICHER VISION:

The development of ethnic minority media in Western democracies

Edited by
Charles Husband

UNESCO Publishing

British Library Cataloguing in Publication Data

Husband, Charles
    A RICHER VISION: The development of ethnic
    minority media in Western democracies
    'Communication and Development' series
    I. Title   II. Series

ISBN: 0 86196 450 0

UNESCO ISBN: 92 3 102941 X

Published in 1994 by
The United Nations Educational, Scientific and Cultural Organization
7, place de Fontenoy, 75352 Paris 07 SP, France
and by
John Libbey & Company Ltd, 13 Smiths Yard, Summerley Street,
London SW18 4HR, England
Telephone: +44 (0)81-947 2777 – Fax: +44 (0)81-947 2664
John Libbey Eurotext Ltd, 6 rue Blanche, 92120 Montrouge, France
John Libbey - C.I.C. s.r.l., via Lazzaro Spallanzani 11, 00161 Rome, Italy

Printed in Great Britain by Whitstable Litho Ltd, Whitstable, Kent, UK

Contents

Acronyms used in the text

ABC	Australian Broadcasting Corporation
ABCB	Australian Broadcasting Control Board
ABT	Australian Broadcasting Tribunal
ACGB	Arts Council of Great Britain
ACOM	Advisory Council for Research on Minorities
ACV	Asian Cinevision
AFC	Australian Film Commission
AFTRS	Australian Film, Television and Radio School
ANPA	American Newspaper Publishers Association
ARA	Association rencontres audiovisuelles
ASNE	American Society of Newspaper Editors
BBC	British Broadcasting Corporation
BET	Black Entertainment Television
BFI	British Film Institute
BRACS	Broadcasting for Remote Aboriginal Communities
BSC	Broadcasting Standards Council
CAAMA	Central Australian Aboriginal Media Association
CAF	Caisse d'allocations familiales
CBS	Columbia Broadcasting System
CCCS	Centre for Contemporary Cultural Studies, Birmingham University
CIEM	Centre d'information et d'études sur les migrations internationales
EEC	European Economic Community
EEO	Equal Employment Opportunity
FAS	Fonds d'action sociale
FFC	Film Finance Corporation
GLC	Greater London Council
IBA	Independent Broadcasting Authority
NATO	North Atlantic Treaty Organization
NESB	Non-English-speaking background
NGO	Non-Governmental Organization
NOS	Dutch National Broadcasting System
NRK	Norwegian Broadcasting Corporation
NWICO	New World Information and Communication Order
OAU	Organization of African Unity
OPEC	Organization of Petroleum Exporting Countries
PBAA	Public Broadcasting Association of Australia
PBF	Public Broadcasting Foundation
PSB	Public Service Broadcasting
RAA	Regional Arts Associations
SBS	Special Broadcasting Service
STOA	Ethnic Minorities' Broadcasting Foundation
UNISAT	Union nationale des institutions sociales d'action pour les Tziganes
VHF	Very high frequency
WRR	Netherlands Scientific Council for Government Policy

Preface

The last three decades have seen significant changes in the representation and employment of ethnic minority populations in the mainstream media of a number of Western democracies in response to pressure from ethnic communities, liberal pressure groups, academics and some non-governmental organizations. Stereotypes in the media have been reduced and in a number of cases it is now possible for ethnic minorities to have access to some media channels. However, much remains to be done.

This study analyses the recent emergence of an ethnic minority media sector within selected national media systems, looking primarily at the development and distribution of technical and professional skills. It is intended as a timely and practical contribution to the overall communications policy debate within which minority media sectors have to survive and develop. In particular, one of the main policy issues forming the background to the debate is the development of anti-discrimination legislation and the articulation of equal opportunities policies. The discussion of both of these is germane to UNESCO's efforts to advance the communication situation of settled migrant communities and ethnic minorities.

UNESCO already has a long history of publishing research on communication, ethnicity and the linked issues of ethnicity and the media. A particular contribution was its support of an international joint study entitled 'The role of information in the realization of the human rights of migrant workers' which brought together media workers, academics and public servants to explore, amongst other concerns, the media needs and rights of migrants and ethnic minorities.

The editor of this study, Charles Husband, who is Professor of Social Analysis in the Department of Social and Economic Studies at Bradford University in the United Kingdom, participated in that research and concluded from it that the role of ethnic minorities as potential creators of mass media material, and agents of mass media production, deserves to be more fully explored. The growing volume of literature on the representation of ethnic minorities by the mass media seemed to be in danger of obscuring a parallel recognition of individuals and ethnic minority communities as the generators of media content. For this reason he agreed to edit this study which illustrates both the vital role of such communities in determining ethnic minority media production and the multiplicity of factors inhibiting the democratization of the mass media so that they reflect multi-ethnic societies more accurately.

The ideas and opinions expressed in this book are those of the authors and do not necessarily represent the views of UNESCO.

Contributors

S.I. Ananthakrishnan has been active in ethnic minority issues in Norway for many years. He has worked on immigration and ethnic minority policies in Norwegian government ministries and is a founder member of the Anti-Racist Centre in Oslo. He has also contributed to a number of international agencies on human rights issues.

Pascale Boucaud is Director of the Institut des Droits de l'Homme at the Université Catholique in Lyon. She has worked extensively on promoting human rights issues in Europe and Africa.

Dr Wiesje Bovenkerk-Teerink is a social psychologist. She was formerly attached to the Dutch Ministry of the Interior where she worked with others in the ethnic minorities department on developing Dutch multi-ethnic policies.

John D.H. Downing is the John T. Jones, Jr. Centennial Professor of Communication in the Radio-Television-Film Department of the University of Texas in Austin. His publications include studies of racism in mainstream American and British media and ethnic minority media in the United States, a study of *The Cosby Show* and work on Third World cinemas.

Charles Husband is Professor of Social Analysis at the University of Bradford. He has a long established research interest in ethnic relations and communications policies. His publications include: *Racism and the Mass Media*, London, Davis-Poynter, 1974, with Paul Hartman; *'Race' in Britain: Continuity and Change*, London, Hutchinson, 1987; *'Race' and Nation*, Perth, Western Australia, Paradigm Press, 1994.

Ali Hussein is an active participant in Black cultural politics in Britain. He is engaged in the independent film production sector and is currently involved in promoting access to film and video production skills.

Matt Ngui is a Malaysian-born Chinese Australian with a BA in Anthropology and a Master's degree in Social Work from the University of Western Australia. He has worked with Australian Commonwealth and State Governments, most recently as Ministerial Adviser on Aboriginal and Multicultural Affairs in Western Australia. He has been awarded a Churchill fellowship to carry out an international comparative study of strategies on community relations in Europe and Asia.

Paul Stubbs is a former lecturer in social work at Bradford University and is now a free-lance researcher working in a number of European countries. His special interests are migration, ethnic mobilization and racism in contemporary Europe.

General introduction: ethnicity and media democratization within the nation-state

Charles Husband

Introduction

This book is not about the representation of ethnic minority persons and communities by the mass media. It does, however, start from a recognition of the power of the media to promote and sustain ideologies of domination and subordination through their representation of ethnic identities, and through the construction of the definition of the situation within which ethnic diversity in society should be understood. The now extensive literature providing a critical deconstruction of the representation of ethnicity through visual imagery and discourse has made the operation of the media in multi-ethnic societies a focus of political concern. Indeed, given the mobility of populations and the transnational nature of much of our contemporary media, this concern has not remained within the domain of the nation-state. There is now a plethora of international instruments and declarations by non-governmental organizations that specifically note the importance of the media in multi-ethnic contexts and seek to outline the media needs and rights of ethnic minority communities. It is in the context of this concern, and in relation to an appreciation of the past and current focus upon media representation of ethnicity, that this book prioritizes the examination of the participation of members of minority communities in the production of print and broadcast media.

The chapters in this book do not attempt to be inclusive; however, through a case-study approach, each one offers an insight into the interaction between the ethnic relations situation and the communications policy in a particular country.

Consequently the chapters below contain a good deal of discussion of the immigration and internal ethnic minority policies of particular states. This discussion is essential; for it is in relation to the specific institutional structures, and politics, of the state that we must examine the communication environment of ethnic minority, and dominant ethnic community, citizens. These chapters clearly illustrate how state policies in relation to immigration, national identity and ethnic diversity shape the framework within which communication policy is formulated and implemented. When linked to a politico-economic analysis of the operation of media within this framework it becomes apparent that the points of leverage in society, from which to articulate and defend ethnic minority communication needs and rights, are weak and vulnerable.

In this introductory chapter I intend to examine some of the conceptual tools that have been routinely applied to the discussion of the operation of media within a democracy. If we start from the de facto reality that migration and settlement have produced new, and contentious, multi-ethnic populations in the states discussed below, we may reasonably ask what role we expect the media to play in such societies. In view of its current visibility in print and conference discourse, the utility of the concept of 'the public sphere' is explored. However, the public sphere is conceived of in relation to the state, and consequently it follows that the nature of this state must itself be problematized. Particularly in relation to multi-ethnic societies, the foundation myths of each nation-state become important in shaping the formal, and popular, understanding of the relation between ethnicity and the 'imagined community' of the nation. I therefore point to the problematic ethnic hegemony that routinely operates within the state, and explore the significance of the state's attempt to define a national identity and culture. These political processes and their significance are further illuminated in the subsequent chapters.

Finally, I explore the ways in which ethnic identities and ethnic political mobilization may be related to the issues of access to, and participation within, the mass media. While the demography of specific ethnic minority communities makes it both viable and necessary to have print and broadcast media operating within community languages, and addressing the particular concerns of these communities, media apartheid cannot be condoned. A public sphere that operates through parallel and exclusive communication systems cannot promote dialogue between fellow citizens. It can facilitate an articulate and informed ethnic self-consciousness within ethnic communities. And it can promote a partisan ethnic political participation within the state. But, even if there were an equity in media resources among ethnic minority groups, which there is not, such a system would always be threatened with political and cultural marginalization by the mainstream media of the dominant ethnic community. This chapter therefore will argue for the empowerment of ethnic minority communities through their participation in mainstream media, as well as through their autonomous production of distinctive media serving specific ethnic audiences and presenting particular communities' perspectives for transmission to others.

The public sphere, citizenship and the nation-state

The notion of the public sphere, outlined by Habermas, (Habermas, 1989; Curran, 1991), provides one useful conceptual template for locating minority media production within a broader context. As Curran notes:

> According to classical liberal theory, the public sphere (or, in more traditional terminology, 'public forum') is the space between government and society in which private individuals exercise formal and informal control over the state: formal control through the election of governments and informal control through the pressure of public opinion. The media are central to this process. They distribute the information necessary for citizens to make an informed choice at election time; they facilitate the formation of public opinion by providing an independent forum of debate; and they enable the people to shape the conduct of government by articulating their views. The media are thus the principal institutions of the public sphere or, in the rhetoric of nineteenth-century liberalism, 'the fourth estate of the realm' (Curran, 1991, p. 29).

Not surprisingly Curran goes on to critique the classical liberal view of the operation of the media. The notion of independent media functioning as neutral conduits for a rich diversity of competing views has a quaint and hollow ring in the light of contemporary mass-media literature. Contemporary debates around the ownership and control of the media point to a concentration of media ownership within the Western European context with a consequent narrowing of interests reflected in the news media and a homogenization of cultural products within broadcast entertainment (Garnham, 1990; Murdock, 1990). Increasing technical sophistication facilitating the reproduction and transmission of information has not had a comparable effect in extending access to information. Indeed there is a strong, if not entirely unqualified, case to the contrary (Schiller, 1989; Melody, 1990). And any hopes that the public service tradition within broadcast media has been an adequate defence against the inexorable operation of market forces must be seriously questioned by the current evidence. Curran (1991) argues of the British situation that, even when informed by the ethos of the public service tradition, broadcasting has functioned as 'an agency privileging dominant discourses and sustaining dominant power groups ...'. And in a more inclusive claim Dahlgren (1991) asserts that:

> In Western Europe public service broadcasting has seen the historical conditions for its existence rapidly dissolving, forcing it to capitulate further to commercial imperatives, with the state contributing to, rather than struggling against, these developments (Dahlgren, 1991, p. 10).

At the same time the state, while remaining actively engaged in seeking to moderate and exploit the media institutions operating within it, is no longer in a position to unambiguously assert its will. The conglomeration and internationalization of media industries have generated systems of production and consumption that transcend the surprisingly permeable economic and cultural boundaries of the nation-state.

Given these cumulative challenges to the operation of the romantic conception of a fluid and open public sphere in contemporary Western Europe, one may ask what purpose the concept may serve. Perhaps as a provocative ideal-type construct to sustain a progressive momentum. As Dahlgren argues:

> The concept of the public sphere must have evocative power, providing us with concrete visions of the democratic society which are enabling rather than disabling. In other words, it must also fuel our utopian imagination, not leave us apathetic or paralytic. *We need to render the public sphere as an object of citizen concern, scrutiny and intervention.* The defence and expansion of the public sphere always remains a political accomplishment (Dahlgren, 1991, p. 9 [emphasis added]).

Citizenship and ethnicity

When we come to consider how the citizen may participate in the public sphere we of course must start from a recognition of the heterogeneity of citizens and their differential access to power. Indeed current discussion of the distinction between 'formal' and 'substantive' citizenship highlights this disparity. Bottomore (1992, p. 66) distinguishes between formal citizenship as simply 'membership of a nation-state' and substantive citizenship as 'an array of civil, political, and especially social rights, involving also some kind of participation in the business of government'. Importantly, as Brubaker (1992) has pointed out, formal citizen status does not guarantee substantive citizenship rights. Indeed in the states discussed below ethnicity has increasingly become a criterion for denying persons with formal citizenship their substantive rights through processes of exclusion and discrimination. Additionally the last decades have seen a growth of ethnic nationalism which has made ethnicity an increasingly significant criterion in the regulation of entry into the state and the granting of formal citizenship.

Citizenship and ethnicity are problematically related to the construction of national agendas within contemporary nation-states. Within the post-colonial experience of many Western European countries there has been a necessary renegotiation of national iconography. The 'glorious past' has had to be re-situated in relation to contemporary political realities. In many instances the historically subordinated, and ethnically differentiated, 'other' defined the superiority of their European rulers through the definitions which were laid upon them (Said, 1978; Kabbani, 1986; Inden, 1990). Geographically distant, and rendered culturally exotic, their identity and labour power could be safely made to serve the interests of their metropolitan masters.

In the post-colonial latter part of the twentieth century such self-serving strategies are no longer so easily sustained. Independent ex-colonies are often now targeted as privileged commercial markets that require a degree of judicious nurturing. And many international economic and political alliances, and their associated institutions, have provided vehicles for a robust exposure of, and challenge to, neo-colonial strategies. The Organization of African Unity, OPEC and the Non-Aligned

Movement; and more recently the ASEAN States, are just some of the possible examples of external points of leverage which contribute to the *realpolitik* to which Western European countries have had to learn to accommodate.

Additionally mass migration of labour in the post-war world has seen the geographical boundaries of national identity fundamentally penetrated as migrant labour has very frequently been transformed into settled ethnic minority populations (Castles, 1984). The external, culturally 'exotic', *other* has for many European countries shattered the literal cordon sanitaire of national boundaries and emerged as a troubling 'internal threat' (Husband, 1987; Taguieff, 1991). In Australia the pragmatic necessity of labour has seen the end of 'the white Australia policy', but not of white Anglo-Celtic hegemonic anxieties (Husband, 1991; Jayasurisa, 1991). In France, the Netherlands and the United Kingdom substantial numbers of people from former colonies have settled in 'the mother country' and challenged the tolerant self-image of those countries. And in a totally different experience, 'Little' Norway with a population of just over four million has in the last decade rehearsed the politics of an 'immigration crisis' that closely echoed that of the United Kingdom in the 1960s and 1970s. Such mass migration has shattered the mythic ethnic homogeneity of contemporary nation-states. Indeed as Máret Sárá points out, in Ananthakrishnan below, new ethnic minority populations may also reveal the presence of the existing ethnic minorities whose problematic existence had been submerged in the prior national consensus.

While the de facto multi-ethnic nature of contemporary Western European nations constitutes a challenge to prior hegemonic cultural agendas, it also exposes the ideological nature of the legal construction of citizenship within each country. Particularities in the historical acquisition of nationhood are reflected in contemporary conceptions of citizenship and nationality. For example, Germany has had a clear conception of national identity linked to a narrow ethnic definition of citizenship. It is an ethnic nation-state within which very large numbers of settled ethnic minority persons are denied citizenship. Yet at the same time the German State recognizes ethnic minority communities and makes some provision to sustain their culture in anticipation of their future return 'home'.

France on the other hand, as a consequence of its unique history, has a strongly demotic-unitarian conception of citizenship in which citizenship is not subject to qualification by gender, ethnicity or religion. So much so that within France the State has difficulty in officially recognizing and responding to the ethnic diversity among its citizenry, many of whom are members of ethnic minorities (see Boucaud & Stubbs below). In comparison the United Kingdom had until the 1981 Nationality Act no legal conception of citizenship in as much as nationals had a common identity as subjects of the Monarch. Thus in regard to the historical relation of the United Kingdom to *her* Commonwealth, it was this common bond with the Monarch that provided the basis for an essentially demotic-unitarian conception of citizenship. However, the escalation of racist responses to immigration into the United Kingdom has moved that nation towards a German model where successive immigration legislation has effectively made access to formal citizenship closely correlated to possession of 'British' ethnic credentials. But given the British Imperial tradition of administering ethnically diverse territories, the United Kingdom has, unlike France, found it to be compatible with her institutional repertoire to create bureaucratic measures to recognize and monitor ethnic diversity among its citizenry (most particularly through the 1968 and 1976 Race Relations Acts).

These examples merely serve to illustrate the very different contexts within which ethnic minority communities may experience their relation to the state and to citizenship rights within it (see Layton-Henry, 1990). They emphasize the 'utopian imagination' that must inform the *specific* application of expectations of the media's role to facilitating citizen participation in the public sphere. Murdock's recent statement on this linkage provides just such a utopian agenda. He argues that:

> We can identify three important ways in which the communications system is implicated in the constitution of citizenship. First, in order for people to exercise their full rights as citizens, they must have access to the information, advice and analysis that will enable them to know what their personal rights are and allow them to pursue them effectively. Second, they must have access to the broadest possible range of information interpretation and debate on areas that involve public political choices, and they must be able to use communications facilities in order to register criticism and propose alternative courses of action. And third, they must be able to recognize themselves and their aspirations in the range of representations on offer within the central communications sectors and be able to contribute to developing and extending these representations.

> To meet these criteria, a communications system needs to be both diverse and open. It must enable a society 'to see its questions and puzzles articulated, its uncomfortable contradictions explored, the half truths and absurdities which it is tempted to believe laughed at, its invisible experiences brought into the light, its marginalized groups allowed a voice' (Mephama, 1990, p. 65). Murdock (1992, p. 21).

One of the problems attendant upon employing an argument that seeks to outline the liberating and progressive potential of the media in relation to maximizing 'citizen rights' is that citizenship is bound to the political entity of the nation-state. As we have already seen, the conceptual baggage that informs the legal and moral expression of citizenship is not independent of the unique history of each nation-state. As a relatively recent manifestation of modernity, the nation-state is a major mechanism of mobilizing and organizing economic and political interests within bounded geographical space and a specific historical time-frame. The geographical boundary of the nation has a historicity of its own, which is routinely refurbished to render the state's very existence normal and invariant. As Hobsbawm and Ranger (1983) have argued, the 'invention of tradition' is an integral task in the nation-state's reproduction of its own continuity. There is then an inherent tension between the invented 'heritage', which roots national identity in *history*, and the change and heterogeneity that characterizes the contemporary Western European nation-state.

The 'imagined community' (Anderson, 1991) of the nation is achieved in relation to the sharing of myths of identity that have in their very emergence been fundamentally dependent upon modern mass media, starting initially with the print media. Consequently an examination of the content of national identity leads to the identification of the interests and mechanisms that were at play in the production of that invented heritage that defines the 'national identity'. These historic blocs are by their very nature anything but representative of the heterogeneity of identities and experience extant among the 'nationals' of the state. Thus the public sphere must engage in an interrogation of the definition of the state itself: an ambitious project.

Schlesinger (1991a), in a valuable analysis of national identity, draws upon Giddens to clarify the distinction between nationalism as 'the cultural sensibility of sovereignty', and the nation-state as an 'administrative and territorially ordered unity.' In Giddens' words:

> What makes 'the nation a necessary element of the nation-state' ... is not the existence of sentiments of nationalism (however strong these may be) but the unification of an administrative apparatus whose power stretches over precisely defined territorial bounds. 'Nationalism', by contrast, may be understood as symbols or beliefs which attribute a communality of experience to the members of a particular regional, ethnic or linguistic category – which may or may not be convergent with the demarcation of a nation-state (Giddens, 1981, p. 13).

In a wonderfully pungent article, Keane elaborates upon the distinction between 'nationalism' and national identity. He caustically points to the centripetal inclusive myopia of nationalism with its attendant self-righteous moral certitudes. Importantly he identifies the awkward relationship between democracy as an ethos and practice within the nation-state, and nationalism as a by-product, and efficient exploiter, of that same democratic system. In his words:

> Nationalism is the child of democratic pluralism – both in the sense that the existence of open state institutions and a minimum of civil liberties enables nationalists to organize and propagate their nationalism, but also in the less obvious sense that democracy breeds insecurity about power and sometimes fear and panic, and, hence, the yearning of some citizens to take refuge in sealed forms of life (Keane, 1992, p. 10).

And where, as will be argued below, the institutions of a multi-ethnic state are appropriated as the hegemonic instruments of dominant ethnic groups, then the processes of political, economic and cultural closure along ethnic boundaries are amplified through the politics of nationalism.

It is immediately apparent that many of the identities available to citizens of a state transcend in their reference the boundaries of the state. Feminism has an inherently international vision, and religion historically, if not in its established institutional forms, markedly challenges the historical arbitrariness of national boundaries. Indeed in the contemporary European context Islam and Christendom are again being constructed as major political rather than 'religious' formations. And in a number of European states Islam is being demonized as threatening, through migration and pan-national identity, the previous certitudes of national-religious identities. Ethnicities too transcend national boundaries in the contemporary world. In reality, ethnic diversity has always been a 'problem' to the homogenizing agenda of nationalism, whether through its defiance of external borders, as in the case of the Sami in Scandinavia, or as a challenge to internal unity, as in that of internal colonialism in the United Kingdom or Black identities in the United States.

The nation, external threat and consolidating ethnic dominance

If ethnic diversity constitutes a political threat to the imagined internal coherence of the nation-state, then developments in satellite technology and the consequences of media deregulation have generated a particular concern with cross-border information flows. A commercial anxiety in relation to the loss of audience share is complemented by cultural anxiety in relation to the alien, and presumed inferior, cultural products which are likely to be imported into the nation's households as a consequence of these new market forces. The European Economic Community and the Council of Europe have provided the institutional frameworks for the rehearsal of just such anxieties. Assuming a common Promethean cultural heritage in 'European Culture', they provided a forum for the national articulation of fears of cultural despoilation to be rehearsed collectively.

Thus nowhere is the inter-national nature of contemporary media institutions revealed in its contradictory complexity better than in relation to the 'European' attempt to regulate the free flow of television across borders. The expansion of new broadcast technologies, particularly in relation to satellite and cable systems, placed in jeopardy the regulatory status quo within state boundaries. At the same time within the European Economic Community there was a political project to build a 'European identity' as the subjective correlate that followed from the border and immigration policies of 'Fortress Europe' (Husband, 1992). As the open market and free flow of labour within the community loomed in 1992, so the member states were vigorously engaged in sealing their borders against the transfrontier 'spillover effect' of the immigration of citizens from 'Third Countries', particularly from 'the south' (see Bunyan, 1991; Webber, 1991). A reified European identity is being forged as a socio-cultural response to the post-colonial European experience; and it is a cultural complement to the projected European 'economic' Community. A strong assertion of this fusion of economic and cultural agendas is found in Schlesinger's statement that:

> In the case of the perspectives of the EC and the Council of Europe on the need to develop a European audio-visual industry, the animating concern has been to use electronic images as a form of cultural-industrial defence against *les défis américain et japonais* of heavy television imports, above all of fictional entertain-

ment. To this end the construction of a strong industrial base for 'European' television production and consumption may function as a kind of cultural cordon sanitaire against foreign values, in which the protective effects on the patient, needless to say, are assumed to be unambiguously edifying (Schlesinger, 1991b, p. 304).

While this statement overly submerges any economic rationale for attempting to regulate a European media market (see Ungerer, 1990), the reality of the cultural agenda is all too evident. And as with the specificity of particular states' politico-cultural conception of citizenship, so too a number of nation-states responded with greater or lesser vehemence to the attempt to use quotas to promote 'European' culture as Hirsch and Peterson (1992) have indicated. However ambiguously, European states sought to mobilize against the perceived threat through both the Council of Europe Convention on Trans-Frontier Television and the European Community Directive, *Television without Frontiers*.

As Tomlinson (1992) has indicated, this invocation of a threat to 'national' and even 'European' culture carries with it a claim to know what that culture is. It is an assertion of a heritage, a canonical cultural repertoire, that is shared by all authentic members. And as he further argues (p. 73), the construction of a discourse in which a threatening cultural 'other' lies beyond the national boundaries can lend a spurious legitimacy to those cultural forces that can assert themselves as representative of 'the nation', or which successfully claim to speak as the national culture. Pieterse in his 1991 article, 'Fictions of Europe', has vigorously rebutted the mythic, Plato-to-NATO, European culture being promoted within the European Economic Community. He sees this enterprise as 'chauvinistic, élitist, pernicious and alienating' (p. 3) in its fabrication of a xenophobic invented heritage, its denial of regional and ethnic minority cultures and its representation of élite culture as culture *tout court*. Certainly the national debates around the need to defend culture against media subversion show a strong core of nationalism rather than a concern to protect and develop the media environment of all citizens within the state. A national identity, as a collective identity, clearly provides a viable discourse for all citizens, whereas nationalism is by nature myopic and exclusionary. However, since national identity is only one, and not necessarily among the most salient, of many identities, then the conflation of nation with culture, and culture with 'heritage', cannot reflect the experience of all citizens. This is particularly so for those whose particular identities are marginalized by such 'traditional' cultural values. Ethnicity, specifically minority ethnicity, routinely constitutes just such a case.

Importantly this marginalization is not confined to the cultural domain, but is also replicated and exacerbated in the economic and political domains. In the era of 'the culture of contentment' (Galbraith, 1992), it seems probable that the wealth of nations is sustained on the shoulders of a structural underclass of low paid and unemployed citizens, a significant segment of which is composed of a disproportionate percentage of each nation's ethnic minority citizens. The discourse of cultural imperialism reveals a terrain of hegemonic struggle. And yet, where that struggle is engaged nation with nation, it does not necessarily represent a progressive agenda that protects the interests of 'second-class citizens'. Nor, as Tomlinson forcefully points out, does defending 'national culture' against a perceived external threat facilitate the recognition and valuing of ethnic diversity within the state.

Ethnicity and the analysis of media environments

Ethnicity is not a fixed property of individuals: it is not an ever-present aspect of their consciousness and behaviour (Rex, 1986). We all achieve our identity in relation to membership of a large number of groups (Tajfel, 1982). Thus at any particular time behaviour will be directed by reference to a particular set of norms rooted in one identity, which is salient in that situation. The footballer on the field is not necessarily influenced by being a plumber or a teacher. A teacher in the class-room is not necessarily influenced by being married, a parent or a tennis player. Similarly, members of ethnic minority communities may also experience themselves in relation to such alternative identities as those based on gender, class, age, caste or religion. At a particular time, in a specific situation, any one of these subjective perspectives might predominate, or act in complex relation to the others. This is what is meant by saying that ethnicity is situational (Wallman, 1986).

The media-related behaviour of members of an ethnic minority community cannot be 'explained' by their ethnicity. They are not merely ethnic, nor is their ethnicity a permanent element of their consciousness. In certain situations they may be acutely aware of their ethnic identity, while in others it may be irrelevant to their thoughts and actions. Consequently members of ethnic communities when watching television may be employing a number of selective filters which reflect, for example, their age, gender and class. This fracturing of media audiences is reflected for example in the ethnic minority press (Phillips-Etenge, 1988) where specific maga-zines have a quite precise target audience in mind. Thus if we speak of 'ethnically relevant' media content, this does not imply that there is an equivalent audience defined solely by their ethnicity. The demonstration of a demand for ethnically relevant media, apparent in the following chapters, indicates the significance of ethnicity within the communication environment of citizens who are also members of ethnic minority communities. A major feature of their communication environ-ment is the co-option of the mainstream media by the dominant ethnic groups (see Husband, 1986).

We can further inhibit any tendency to stereotype audiences as 'ethnic', and only ethnic, by noting the heterogeneity within ethnic communities. One aspect of the cultural politics of subordinated ethnic minority communities has been the asser-tion of various forms of essentialist definitions of their ethnicity. This may be consist-ent with attempting to construct in-group solidarity, but, as Black feminists have pointed out in relation to gender politics, such essentialism constitutes yet another form of oppression. And it is a denial of difference that is doubly pernicious since it is empowered within the ethnic community by its asserted roots in challenging exter-nal oppression. As one author has recently argued:

Contemporary critiques of essentialism (the assumption that there is a black essence shaping all African-American experience, expressed traditionally by the concept of 'soul') challenge the idea that there is only 'one' legitimate black experience. Facing the reality of multiple black experiences enables us to develop diverse agendas for unification, taking into account the specificity and diversity of who we are (hooks, 1991, p. 37).

In relation to media policies it is critical that this diversity of experience and identities be assiduously retained within any analytic model employed. Thus, where states develop ethnic minority media strategies, as for example in the case of Australia and the Netherlands below, there is a need to monitor the role of the state in specifying the ethnic categories that are recognized within its policies. These may privilege specific identities and operate with imposed conceptions of ethnic identities that are functionally meaningless for those located within them, such as 'Asian' in the United Kingdom and 'Non-English-Speaking Background' in Australia.

Equally it is important to consider the implications of specific ethnic identities in regard to the particular tensions they may generate in relation to attempts to forge united fronts against common experiences of the dominant ethnic community as racist and exploitative. 'Women of colour', as defined by Mohanty (1991, p. 7), and the idea of 'blackness', as defined by Grewal *et al.* (1988, p. 1), in the British context are both powerful demonstrations of the very considerable, and real, ethnic diversity that, it is hoped, will form 'a viable oppositional alliance' through 'a common context of struggle'. There is ample evidence of the power of ethnic factionalism to undermine such collective oppositional strategies. In the United Kingdom, Muslim communities are currently questioning the efficacy of 'black' politics in relation to their specific needs (Modood, 1990), while within Australia the Aboriginal and 'Non-English-Speaking-Background' communities pursue independent struggles against the 'Anglo-Celtic' hegemony.

Of course it is overly simplistic to oppose narrow ethnic mobilization to oppositional alliances. The two may operate simultaneously, though be focused around different domains of struggle that engage with different popular constituencies and state institutions. Ethnicity should not be understood only as 'consciousness of kind' but also in relation to the institutional infrastructure that facilitates the possibility of expressing identity through culturally-valued activity. It was Barth (1969) who shifted attention from a fascination with ethnicity as common culture – the 'Ain't they quaint' ethnographies – to a concern with the mechanisms of boundary maintenance. This requires of us a complementary shift from the social psychology of identity to the political economy of institutional power vested in, inter alia, commerce, the law and the media.

Within the same state different ethnic minority communities may well have an equivalent sense of 'consciousness of kind' and yet have access to very different media environments through which to articulate and defend that identity. There is consequently always a necessary struggle for the control of media in a multi-ethnic society. As Brass has observed, this competition for resources is multifaceted:

> Ethnic identity formation is viewed as a process that involves three sets of struggles. One takes place within the ethnic group itself for control over its material and symbolic resources, which in turn involves defining the group's boundaries and its rules for inclusion and exclusion. The second takes place between ethnic groups as a competition for rights, privileges, and available resources. The third takes place between the state and the groups that dominate it, on the one hand, and the populations that inhabit its territory (Brass, 1985, p. 1).

Thus we see in the following chapters the way in which mainstream media institutions are predominantly staffed by members of the dominant ethnic groups whose networks and institutional practices contribute to the exclusion and marginalization of ethnic minority personnel. We also see evidence of the way in which patriarchy operates within this system, thereby adding a further dimension to the processes of exclusion. There is an indication too of the competition between ethnic groups for access to media resources, as for example in the case of Radio Immigranten (see Chapter 5).

The increasing diversity of media research perspectives has progressively pointed to the necessity of conceptualizing the relation of media and audience in a complex multi-layered manner. The rejection of the spectre of the passive, and pacified, mass audience has made way for the confident celebration of the actively interpretative social agent (e.g. Ang, 1991). And far from being an isolated media consumer, the individual's encounter with the mass media must be located within the specificity of his or her own milieu and its contingent, 'everyday' realities (e.g. Morley, 1986). As a corrective to the earlier simplicities of media analysis, this contemporary complexity is to be welcomed. But it should not be allowed to celebrate difference and agency at the expense of neglecting, or obscuring, the continuing relevance of macro-analyses of, for example, the political economy of media institutions and the hegemonic significance of media production. Something of the tension in analysis I am pointing to is contained in Dahlgren's statement that:

> These newer intellectual currents alert us to important considerations such as the subject as a site of negotiation and contestation. Meaning is thus never fully fixed. Incorporating this insight with the polysemic character of media discourses and audience interpretations has important consequences ... which cannot be explored here. Suffice to say that among the more challenging questions to which these currents give rise is to specify the possibilities and limits of the 'free play' of sense-making in relation to the systemic character of social structure and ideology (Dahlgren, 1991, p. 19).

It is precisely through the determination of 'the possibilities and limits of the free-play of sense-making' that contemporary nation-states seek to negotiate the imagined community of the nation, and reproduce the sensibilities that are consistent with it. And the issue of media-facilitated cultural imperialism remains a political issue precisely because autonomous subjects cannot of themselves transcend the pernicious limitations of the structured social spaces that they occupy. It is in relation to a clear conception of the structural location of ethnic minorities in society that analysis of media content may reveal the fine-grained textures of containment and imaginative sclerosis that are the ideological correlates of specific social relations. Post-colonial critics of the Western representation of 'the other' are already revealing the value of such a political project (see, for example, Gates, 1987; Inden, 1990; Kabbani, 1986; Minh-Ha, 1991; Mohanty *et al.*, 1991; Sharabi, 1990).

Let me extend this point, and develop my concern, by suggesting that there are equally ambiguous possibilities inherent in developments in another area of analysis. Within the literature on ethnicity there has been for too long a history of 'blaming the victim' (Ryan, 1971) and of pathologizing ethnic minority cultures (e.g. CCCS, 1982). Consequently it is important to recognize the repertoires of resistance that have been part of the subordinated ethnic minority cultures. And there is now no lack of texts that assert the modalities of experience and expression which have characterized these repertoires of resistance, and continue to do so. However, I am anxious lest these descriptions be reduced to celebrations, and that consequently a righteous capacity for resistance to oppression becomes transmuted in liberal quarters into a perceived momentum sufficient of itself to lead to equity. The celebration of a people's capacity for resistance can too easily contribute to a willing avoidance of engaging with the specific realities of their contemporary subordination. An empathetic admiration for a people's struggle can obscure one's continued participation in their exploitation. Gouldner's (1973) scathing critique of 'feel good' ethnographies of the 'underdog' continues to have relevance today as societies generate the research to interpret their multi-cultural condition (see Bovenkerk-Teerink below).

To bring this point to a close let me contemplate a fusion of these two 'currents'. A fusion of the vision of the actively hermeneutic audience within their bounded community of resistance could unfortunately generate an overly optimistic vision of the media politics of multi-ethnic societies. At an extreme, since audiences are doomed to consume and decode media within the unique and potent domain of their subculture, then any concern about ethnic hegemony within society may be seen as the overheated anxieties of a leftist old guard. Or, given the view of fragmented media audiences operating with particular receptive codes, then concern about racism and the media may be 'legitimately' reduced to a focus upon a relatively few vulnerable, or extremist, demographic entities. And consequently a concern with the ubiquitous ideological reproduction of racism, or homophobia or patriarchy becomes labelled as a perverse, and 'political', neurosis.

In order to address the active and institutional racism and xenophobic exclusionary practices that are revealed in the following chapters, it is clearly necessary to seek to reveal the mechanisms that determine the possibilities and limits of the 'free play' of sense-making.

Conclusion

There is now a very considerable literature revealing the stereotypical and ideological representation of ethnic minorities in the mass media. The analysis of this misrepresentation continues to be politically necessary, and is being carried out with ever-increasing sophistication. A study of the representation of ethnic minorities by the media often reveals more about the product than the process that produced it. It is now essential that research energies should be applied to examining the situation of ethnic minorities as active agents in media production; for it is clear that ethnic minorities are marginalized not only through media images but through their exclusion from full and equitable participation in media industries. The following chapters illuminate something of these processes in addressing the fundamental question of access to, and participation in, the mass media by members of ethnic minority communities.

The necessity of ensuring, and enabling, ethnic minority media activity has been recognized in many international declarations and agreements that highlight the centrality of communication in achieving fundamental human rights. Hujanen (1984) provides a listing of such statements which formed the backdrop to a UNESCO supported programme on 'The Role of Information in the Realization of the Human Rights of Migrant Workers.' That programme itself generated an important body of comparative literature, and elaborated upon the policy requirements that were consistent with a concern with the democratization of communication (see Hujanen, 1986, 1988, 1989). International statements in this area continue to proliferate as for example in the Council of Europe's *Colloquy on Migrants, Media and Cultural Diversity* (1988) and the final report of The Community Relations Project in 1991 entitled *Community and Ethnic Relations in Europe*. Further support for asserting the rights of ethnic minorities, and for affirmative action to remedy inequity is to be found in *The International Convention on the Elimination of all Forms of Racial Discrimination* (see Meron, 1985). Such international instruments and policy statements are important in providing a framework for asserting ethnic minority rights and in providing a benchmark against which to demonstrate their routine denial.

In view of the foregoing we should be sceptical about the willingness of states to enforce these declarations and about media industries' interest in recognizing their significance. Since national immigration policy and border control inform internal 'minority' policies, as the chapters below demonstrate, there has to be an independent focus of leverage outside the state. Thus autonomous minority media constitute a critical element of the media environment of multi-ethnic societies.

Downing's (1984) study of radical media raises a number of pertinent points about the structure and operation of alternative, small-scale media. As with the examples in this text, he points to the fact that the financial organization of the cases he studied 'had been a major problem for most of them, and in many cases ... a nettle grasped most reluctantly' (p. 352). The separation of these two points is important. It is clear that many ethnic minority media enterprises are seriously impaired in their operation because of financial constraints, and this very fact makes financial acumen an essential skill within such organizations. A politically naïve reduction of ethnic minority media expertise to 'counter-cultural creativity' evokes, and requires, a media environment devoid of financial imperatives. The survival and expansion of ethnic minority media activity requires, and must value, the specific contribution of ethnic minority financial and managerial expertise. At times it seems that the majority media, and satellite ethnic minority media, are successfully advancing a 1990s hi-tech refurbished 'Sambo' image in which ethnic minority media 'names' are celebrated as film directors, rap artists, authors and musicians: creative artists all. Ethnic creativity is highly saleable in contained, economically colonized, cultural markets. Realistically these cross-over points of cultural production with majority/minority audiences must be occupied by ethnic minority artists, some proportion of whom will retain a capacity to protect their own personal and ethnic integrity through their work: as indeed many do. But part of the contribution to building ethnic minority media is the building of an economic and institutional structure outside those of the dominant majority. There is consequently a need to nurture managerial and production skills within the ethnic minority media communities.

A related point arising from Downing's study is his assertion that 'media democracy works, and [that it] takes various forms' (p. 355). The case-studies he records demonstrate a variety of open management structures that challenge the inevitability of the extremely hierarchical managerial structures which predominate in mainstream media. Open and flexible management structures are an essential factor in the provision of responsive and responsible media as outlined by Dahlgren (1991) and Murdock (1992) above. However, Downing adds a very important qualification to this account of internal democracy in noting that:

> Internal democracy in mass media is only a step, however important, toward democratizing communications. Without an open relationship with constructive popular forces, internal democracy has a very limited utility indeed. What would be the value of an all-white male middle class media democracy in the US? (Downing, 1984, p. 355).

One of the implications of this statement for ethnic minority media is that a self-perpetuating coterie of individuals, even operating within an organizational structure of considerable internal democracy, is hardly likely to reflect and represent the heterogeneity that exists within all ethnic communities, i.e. a heterogeneity that is characterized by differentiation in terms of *inter alia* gender, class, age, sexual preference and health. As we have seen, Black feminist writers such as hooks (1991) and Mohanty *et al.* (1991) have eloquently exposed the dangers of essentialist definitions of ethnic identity. Consequently ethnic minority media structures ideally require both open internal management structures and highly developed avenues for routine access to the diversity of experience represented within their communities. We need to be clear that we need autonomous ethnic minority media which can speak for, and to, their own community; ethnic minority media which can generate a dialogue between ethnic minority communities; and between these and dominant ethnic community audiences.

However, mainstream media industries must remain a target for change, and the ploy of having highly visible ethnic minority broadcasters fronting for an institution in which they are singularly absent from executive positions cannot be tolerated (see Downing & Ngui below). The dangers of an ethnic minority media ghetto are clearly signalled by Bovenkerk-Terrink in the following pages, and yet the answer is not to abandon specific provision for ethnic minority audiences nor solely by expanding an independent ethnic minority media sector. The removal of discrimination within the mainstream media and a readily permeable interface between mainstream and ethnic minority media are basic requirements of the media industries in multiethnic societies.

The following chapters highlight the existence of successful ethnic minority media, and of a growing challenge to the institutional racism of mainstream media. That challenge is present in the individual drive, expertise and persistence of ethnic minority media workers and professionals, just as it is in the commercial possibilities of significantly large ethnic minority audiences; it is in the exploitation of cable, satellite and video cassette recorders to reject ethnically alien mainstream media, in the growing potential of transnational audience and production networks, and in the unwillingness of members of 'dominant' ethnic communities to deny the communication rights of fellow citizens. The struggle to achieve equity in the media industries for ethnic minority persons and communities is an assertion of the communication rights of all persons: media democratization cannot be pursued within a media 'apartheid'. The aim must be one of a richer vision for all.

References

Ang, I. (1991): *Desperately Seeking the Audience*. London, Routledge.

Bottomore, T. (1992): Citizenship and Social Class, Forty Years On. In: T.H. Marshall, T.Bottomore. *Citizenship and Social Class*. London, Pluto Press.

Brass, P.R. (1985): Ethnic Groups and the State. In: P.R. Brass (ed.). *Ethnic Groups and the State*. Beckenham, Croom Helm.

Brubaker, W.R. (1992): *Citizenship and Nationhood in France and Germany*. New York, Monthly Review Press.

Bunyan, T. (1991): Toward an Authoritarian Europe State. *Race and Class*, Vol. 32, January–March, pp. 19–27.

Castles, S. (1984): *Here for Good*. London, Pluto Press.

Centre for Contemporary Cultural Studies (1982): *The Empire Strikes Back*. London, Hutchinson.

Curran, J. (1991): Rethinking the media as public sphere. In: P.Dahlgren, C. Sparks, op. cit.

Dahlgren, P. & Sparks, C. (1991): Op. cit., Introduction.

Dahlgren, P. & Sparks, C. (1991): *Communication and Citizenship*. London, Routledge.

Downing, J. (1984): *Radical Media*. South End Press.

Ford Report, European Parliament Session Documents (1990): Report on behalf of the Committee of Inquiry in Racism and Xenophobia, A3–195/90.

Galbraith, J.K. (1992): *The Culture of Contentment*. London, Sinclair-Stevenson.

Garnham, N. (1990): *Capitalism and Communication*. London, Sage.

Gates, H.L. (1987): *Figures in Black*. Oxford, Oxford University Press.

Giddens, A. (1981): *A Contemporary Critique of Historical Materialism*. London, Macmillan.

Gouldner, A.W. (1973): The Sociologist as Partisan. In: A.W. Gouldner. *For Sociology*. London, Allen Lane.

Grewal, S., Kay, J., Landor, L., Lewis, G. & Parmar, P. (1988): *Charting the Journey*. London, Sheba Feminist Publishers.

Habermas, J. (1989): *The Structural Transformation of the Public Sphere*. Cambridge, Polity Press.

Hancock, A. (1992): *Communication Planning Revisited*. Paris, UNESCO.

Hirsch, M. & Peterson, V. (1992): Regulating of Media at the European Level. In: K. Siune, W. Truetzschler (eds.). *Dynamics of Media Politics*. London, Sage.

Hobsbawm, E.J. & Ranger, T. (eds.). (1983): *The Invention of Tradition*. Cambridge, Cambridge University Press.

hooks, b. (1991): *Yearning*. London, Turnaround Press.

Hujanen, T. (1984): *The Role of Information in the Realization of the Human Rights of Migrant Workers*. Lausanne, Bureau lausannois pour les immigrés.

Hujanen, T. (1984): *The Role of Information in the Realization of the Human Rights of Migrant Workers*. Report of International Conference, 1983. University of Tampere, Department of Journalism and Mass Communication.

Hujanen, T. (1986): *The Role of Information in the Realization of the Human Rights of Migrant Workers*. Progress Report of Joint Study. University of Tampere, Department of Journalism and Mass Communication.

Hujanen, T. (1988): *The Role of Information in the Realization of the Human Rights of Migrant Workers*. Conclusions and Recommendations. University of Tampere, Department of Journalism and Mass Communication.

Hujanen, T. (1989): *Information, Communication and the Human Rights of Migrants*. Lausanne, Bureau lausannois pour les immigrés.

Husband, C. (1986): Mass media, communication policy and ethnic minorities. In: *Mass Media and the Minorities*. Paris, UNESCO.

Husband, C. (1986): Multiculturalism as Official Policy in Australia. In: R. Nile, op. cit.

Husband, C. (1992): *Minorities, Mobility and Communication in Europe*. Research and Policy Paper, No. 2, Spring 1992. University of Bradford, Race Relations Research Unit.

Inden, R. (1990): *Imagining India*. Oxford, Blackwell.

Jayasuriya, L. (1991): Citizenship, Democratic Pluralism and Ethnic Minorities in Australia. In: R. Nile, op. cit.

Kabbani, R. (1986): *Europe's Myths of Orient*. London, Macmillan.

Keane, J. (1989): 'Liberty of the Press' in the 1980s. *New Formations*, No. 8, Summer.

Keane, J. (1992): Democracy's poisonous fruit. In: *The Times Literary Supplement*, No. 4664, Aug. 1992, pp. 10–12.

Layton-Henry, Z. (1990): *The Political Rights of Migrant Workers in Western Europe*. London, Sage.

Maggiore, M. (1990): *Audiovisual Production in the Single Market*. Commission of the Europe Communities, CB–58–90–481-EN-C.

McQuail, D. & Siune, K. (eds.) (1986): *New Media Politics*. London, Sage.

Melody, W. (1990): Communication policy in the global information society : whither the public interest? In: M. Ferguson (ed.). *Public Communication: The New Imperatives*. London, Sage.

Mephama, J. (1990): The Ethics of Quality Television. In: G. Mulgan. *The Question of Quality*. London, British Film Institute Publishing, pp. 56–72.

Meron, T. (1985): The Meaning and Reach of the International Convention on The Elimination of all Forms of Racial Discrimination. *American Journal of International Law*, 79, pp. 283–318.

Minh-Ha, T.T. (1991): *When the Moon Waxes Red*. London, Routledge.

Modood, T. (1990): British Asian Muslims and the Rushdie Affair. *Political Quarterly*, 61 (2).

Mohanty, C.T., Russo, A. & Torres, L. (1991): *Third World Women and the Politics of Feminism*. Bloomington, Indiana University Press.

Morley, D. (1986): *Family Television : Cultural Power and Domestic Leisure*. London, Comedia.

Murdock, G. (1990): Redrawing the map of the communications industries: concentration and ownership in the era of privatization. In: M. Ferguson (ed.). *Public Communication: The New Imperatives*. London, Sage.

Murdock, G. (1992): Citizens, consumers and public culture. In: M. Skovmand, K. C. Schroder, op. cit., pp. 17–42.

Nile, R. (ed.). (1991): *Immigration and the Politics of Ethnicity and Race in Australia and Britain*. Carlton, Bureau of Immigration Research.

Nordenstreng, K. (1984): *The Mass Media Declaration of UNESCO*. Norwood, New Jersey, Ablex.

Phillips-Etenge, E. (1988): *Black British Consumer Markets*. London, The Planner's Guide.

Pieterse, J.N. (1991): Fictions of Europe. *Race and Class*, op. cit., pp. 3–10.

Rex, J. (1986): *Race and Ethnicity*. Milton Keynes, Open University Press.

Rex, J. & Mason, D. (1986): *Theories of Race and Ethnic Relations*. Cambridge, Cambridge University Press.

Ryan, W. (1971): *Blaming The Victim*. New York, Pantheon.

Said, E.W. (1979): *Orientalism*. New York, Vintage Books.

Schiller, H. (1989): *Culture Inc: The Corporate Takeover of Public Expression*. New York, Oxford University Press.

Schlesinger P. (1991a): On National Identity. Part 2: Collective Identity in Social Theory. In: P. Schlesinger, *Media, State and Nation*. London, Sage.

Schlesinger P. (1991b): Media, the Political Order and National Identity. *Media Culture and Society*, Vol. 13, No. 3, pp. 297–308.

Sharabi, H. (1990): *Theory, Politics and the Arab World*. London, Routledge.

Skovmand, M. & Schroder, K.C. (eds.) (1992): *Media Cultures: Reappraising Transnational Media*. London, Routledge.

Taguieff, P.-A. (1991): *Face au racisme* (2 Vols.). Paris, Éditions La Découverte.

Tajfel, H (1982):. *Social Identity and Intergroup Relations*. Cambridge, Cambridge University Press.

Tomlinson, J. (1992): *Cultural Imperialism*. London, Pinter Publishers.

Ungerer, H. (1990): *Telecommunications in Europe*. Commission of the Europe Communities, CM–59–90–346-EN-C.

Wallman, S. (1986): The Application of Anthropological Theory to the Study of Boundary Processes. In: D. Mason; J. Rex, op. cit..

Webber, F. (1991): From ethnocentrism to Euro-racism. *Race and Class*, op. cit., pp. 11–18.

1

Communications training programmes for members of ethnic minority groups in the USA: an overview

John D.H. Downing

Introduction

This report presents its findings in three sections: (1) A summary account of employment and promotion patterns of ethnic minority groups in the various sectors of the United States communications industry; (2) A similarly brief presentation of recruitment and retention policies, with particular reference to the case-studies offered by the operation of some specific programmes; (3) Certain common themes emerging from interviews with individuals enjoying direct personal knowledge of these programmes, and of the current climate and personnel practices in the communications industry.

However, it is necessary to make an initial observation. Nationally, the climate has altered over the 1980s and into the 1990s with regard to serious projects for ethnic minority hiring and promotion across the entire economy. Both the Reagan and the Bush Administrations signalled very publicly and in numerous ways their rejection of affirmative action strategies. Instances include their appointments of justices to such bodies as the United States Supreme Court, to the whole range of lower Federal courts and to the Federal Civil Rights Commission; their presidential vetoes of civil rights legislation passed by Congress; and, not least, Mr Bush's approving appointment to the post of Chairman of the Republican National Committee of the late Mr Lee Atwater, his former campaign manager, and progenitor of a key TV advertisement in the 1988 Presidential race. The commercial in question was no ordinary one. It centred upon a paroled Black rapist as an object-lesson in the dangers of voting for other than Republican candidates. The advertisement, played and re-played countless times nationally, pandered to and consecrated the deepest racial fears and antagonisms of White communities. To understand the impact these and other actions had in the United States, it is necessary to recognize not only the willingness of many individuals, equally commonly observed in Western Europe and Australia, to leave the racial status quo intact, but also the powerful agenda-setting function of American Presidents over policies and public discourse in the domestic arena.

Not only has this influence operated in the formal judicial setting, but it has helped to reduce public readiness to undertake the *effort* to make affirmative action programmes work. Indeed, by the close of 1990, in part thanks to the Bush Administration's repeated rejection of cautiously framed bi-partisan anti-discrimination legislation passed by Congress, the word 'quotas' had become a code term in public political/racial discourse in the United States signifying rejection of affirmative action programmes for ethnic minority groups. An energetic and non-racist Governor of Mississippi lost a gubernatorial election in November 1991 to his conservative opponent precisely on this issue. In 1992, Harvey Gantt, Democratic senatorial candidate from North Carolina, and an African-American, lost to ultra-conservative incumbent Jesse Helms as a result of being portrayed by Helms' TV commercials as in favour of job-quotas. Former KKK leader David Duke won a very substantial vote in the Louisiana gubernatorial election in significant measure because of identifying himself with opposition to racial quotas. Though these instances are from the South of the United States, it would be a gross error to see them as merely regional in implication.

Thus in assessing the effectiveness of media training projects for members of ethnic minority groups it becomes all the harder at a distance to dissociate appearance from reality, to disentangle public relations claims about such programmes from actual experience of them by those who pass through them. It is not that previous presidential administrations, with the partial exception of the Johnson Administration, swung the helm significantly towards the realization of ethnic minority progress, but simply that the tone they set was much less aggressively dismissive of African-American and Hispanic American needs at large, Bush's occasional appointment of a Colin Powell or a Clarence Thomas to a key post having little or no impact on these needs.

The United States remains a very populous and complex society, and mercifully the negative political force I have identified is countered at a number of points by individuals who are both committed to racial justice and energetic in organizing long-haul strategies to approach its realization. There are some illuminating stories to be told on the positive as well as the negative side. But their prevalence should not be exaggerated.

Lastly, by way of introduction, let me cite Dorothy Butler Gilliam, *Washington Post* columnist, who has pointed out the disastrous consequences of perpetuating the present imbalance in the presence of ethnic minorities in the higher levels of communication organizations: 'The cataclysmic changes in Eastern Europe have increasingly made the United States the democratic model for a world in which large regions are threatened by ethnic conflict and nationalistic aspirations. To fill its leadership role, the United States has to establish within its own borders a new social paradigm, one that recognizes diversity as a cultural and political asset rather than a problem or, worse, a tool for self-serving political interests' (Gilliam, 1991, p. 134).

Employment and promotion patterns: an outline

Data on the employment and promotion of members of ethnic minority groups in the United States communications industry are of greatly different quality depending upon which branch of the industry is in focus. The most detailed data available are on print media, followed by electronic media. The reason is that the American Newspaper Publishers Association (ANPA) and the American Society of Newspaper Editors (ASNE) have both sponsored thorough research, have established bureaux of minority affairs and have set affirmative-action hiring goals for print media. Similarly, the Federal Communications Commission and the National Association of Broadcasters (the broadcast industry association and lobby group) have also conducted systematic research on the issue, the latter through its Office of Minority Services. The lesson is worth noting before moving on: without this type of institutional commitment on the part of the relevant industry bodies, information 'first base' is virtually impossible to reach (unless, of course, a government department is mandated to collect and diffuse such data).

When it comes to the other sectors of the industry, information becomes extremely hard to acquire, especially systematic information. Whether in advertising, public relations, film, telecommunications, or media management, the data are still mostly rather thin, with public relations being the best researched, due mainly to the efforts, not of a professional association, but of a single academic researcher, Professor Marilyn Kern-Foxworth of Texas A&M University. There is a very pressing need for initial and ongoing research funds to begin to establish patterns and trends of ethnic minority employment in all these other major sectors.

Let us, however, establish what we can in each of these seven branches of the communications industry, recalling throughout that ethnic minorities form nearly one quarter (22 per cent) of the total American civilian labour force. If legal and immigration categories are set aside, then undocumented foreign workers would noticeably boost this percentage.

Print media

According to a 1990 national survey commissioned by ANPA and whose results were made available to the public in June that year, ethnic minorities composed 18 per cent of the newspaper industry workforce, compared to a 1988 figure of 16 per cent. However, it is very important to disaggregate this figure into its constituent elements. The sector with the largest percentage, 25 per cent, was circulation, which had also grown the fastest over the previous two years (from 19 per cent). The sector with the smallest percentage was news/editorial, with 10 per cent, and in this sector there had been no change over the previous two years. Furthermore, ethnic minority group executives in the news/editorial category constituted only 5 per cent of those in such positions. Perhaps not surprisingly, the best opportunity for executive rank seemed to be in circulation, with 13 per cent being from ethnic minority groups.

Thus it was clear from any precise delineation of the distribution of employees that print journalists as such, especially editors, were overwhelmingly White, and that the best chances of employment for ethnic minorities were in handling newsprint at unsocial hours in the middle of the night.

Electronic media

Ethnic minority group members constituted 17.1 per cent of all broadcast employees in 1989, according to figures supplied to the researcher by the National Association of Broadcasters, up from 14.4 per cent in 1980. However, as I observed in a previous essay on this topic (Downing, 1988a, p. 98f), and as others have noted before and since, the Federal Communications Commission categories for broadcast employees are framed in such a way that determining executive rank is impossible from their figures. In 1987, for example, fully 85 per cent of all broadcast employees were defined as Officials and Managers, Professionals, Technicians or Sales Workers. None the less, it is widely acknowledged that the prominence of ethnic minority TV newscasters sadly is in inverse ratio to their presence at executive desks.

As regards the cable industry, initial figures seem slightly more encouraging. In 1987, ethnic minority group members constituted 19.5 per cent of cable industry employees (Downing, 1988a, p. 100). But once again, the concentration of their employment was in the least-paid and least influential category, namely office sales, and their scarcity was most marked in the professional category. Moreover it should not be disregarded that labour deployment in the cable industry is pared to the bone, with pay-levels generally to match. The cash-rich cable companies guard their bank balances very jealously indeed.

Public relations

From the research of Kern-Foxworth (1989a; 1989b), it appears that out of a total labour-force of about 150,000, just under 11,000 (7.3 per cent) were members of ethnic minority groups. Just 35 out of around 4,000 public relations professionals accredited by the Public Relations Society of America were from this sector of society. Furthermore, her studies showed that the aspects of the profession with the most authority, pay and prestige, namely the consultative dimensions, were least likely to be occupied by ethnic minority group members, who were in turn far more predictably to be found spending their time turning out newsletters and press-releases, the so-called 'communication technician' roles. The larger the organization in this professional field, the less likely were such individuals to have gravitated into the more senior positions. This latter pattern was also found to be true of public relations employees in government organizations, which numerically speaking employed a slightly disproportionate percentage (25 per cent) of ethnic minority group members. Finally, Kern-Foxworth established a $16,000 average differential in pay between the 348 mid-level ethnic minority professionals she interviewed, and the pay-rate for that level in the industry as a whole.

Advertising, telecommunications, film, management

Advertising, as indicated, has been one of the under-researched areas. One reason may well be the attitudes of many top executives, as Bushnell (1990) discovered when she tried to research the issue. The major agencies mostly either refused to comment, or ignored repeated telephone calls on the subject. The impression of those members of ethnic minority groups in the industry whom she interviewed, including those who had set up their own small firms, was that many agency staff were either ignorant of, or sometimes overtly hostile towards, ethnic minorities. As one Black freelance producer with experience of some major agencies put it: 'I believe the advertising industry is one of the most racist in this country' (Bushnell, 1990, p. 50).

The same might certainly be said of the telecommunications industry. Again, unfortunately, there are only impressionistic data. However, from this researcher's own experience of attending large New York City meetings of telecom executives, and of discussing the issue with professionals and researchers familiar with the industry, it appears to be an overwhelmingly White male bastion.

The areas of film, and of communications management, are just as obscure for present purposes. When the NAACP was preparing a report on ethnic minority employment in Hollywood film and television, none of the four TV networks were prepared to supply precise employment statistics from their files. These were only provided by Warner Brothers and Walt Disney among the major film studios, although five other film studios offered written reports on their hiring patterns. This type of arrogance in refusing data on a matter of ongoing major public concern is hard to disregard as an index of basic policy on ethnic minority hiring. Data supplied by some of the key guilds which control access to employment indicated that, as of 1987, ethnic minority group members constituted 3 per cent of the Writers Guild of America, 8 per cent of the Screen Actors Guild, and 2 per cent of the Directors Guild of America (*Out of Focus Out of Sync,* 1991, pp. 21–22, 27). There is just one agency, TRIAD, specializing in Black applicants. The best figures of any employment category were in the union local for Theatrical Stage Employees, which had a 15 per cent Black membership. These occupations focused on props, carpentry, scenery, lighting and sound; not the top end of the process, however essential to it.

In 1991, there was a sudden plethora of films directed by Black artists and with largely or entirely Black casts and themes. This was a welcome if abrupt switch in Hollywood's readiness to fund minority artists' endeavours, and was at the time of writing unaccompanied by a similar extension of opportunity to film artists from other ethnic groups. However, it should not be overlooked that these films were made on rather picayune budgets by Hollywood traditions, and that in some cases the marketing of the films was underfunded and inept, with the result that some quite unnecessarily made a loss. Furthermore, with no minority presence to speak of at the executive level (*Out of Focus – Out of Sync*, 1991, p. 17), such a sudden 'wave' of films can be cancelled very easily. *Première* magazine (May 1991) listed the 100 top power brokers in Hollywood, of whom Eddie Murphy was twenty-second and Spike Lee sixty-seventh. No other non-Anglos were listed. In the financially strapped world of independent film and video, there was a growing presence of Asian-American directors. It may be that in future this cohort will gravitate, at least in part, into mainstream film-making, but for the present this is rarely the case.

In the case of communications management, again the only systematic data available are for the newspaper industry. Here in the 1990 ANPA survey referred to above, ethnic minority group members numbered 9 per cent of the executives in accounting and finance, 7 per cent in advertising, 7 per cent in general management and administration, 11 per cent in information systems and services, 10 per cent in marketing, promotion and research and 11 per cent in production. (The figures for the two remaining areas, news/editorial and circulation, were cited above.)

Thus it can be concluded without difficulty that there is a very long way to go before ethnic minority groups are adequately represented at all levels of the communications industry in the United States. Let us turn now to an examination of some of the programmes and projects designed to alleviate this entrenched racial inequity.

Training programmes for members of ethnic minority groups

A systematic survey of these programmes, and an assessment of their experience and effectiveness, would be a very valuable undertaking. As indicated in the Introduction, there would be some considerable complexity attached to the investigation because of the difficulty in a number of instances of establishing the reality behind a certain public relations gloss. The other research difficulty would consist in mapping the enormous variety of such programmes across the United States. We may provisionally divide such projects into three categories: industry internships for high school and university students; undergraduate and graduate college programmes of academic study of communications (to which may be appended the role of college newspapers and broadcast stations); and the ethnic minority sector of the media industry. Some further comments on each are in order at this point, but the first thing to note is that many of these programmes may at times have members of ethnic minority groups in them without necessarily catering specifically to them.

A common feature of American communications industries is their use of interns, namely people working for a stipulated number of hours per week, generally about twenty, over a set period of time, rarely less than six weeks in duration. These individuals may be paid or unpaid. They may or may not receive academic credit towards graduation (normally ungraded credits) as a result of their successful participation in the programme. Pay is much rarer than the reverse, and paid internships which also gain credit are very rare, not least because they would be discountenanced by many academic institutions.

The content of these internships varies tremendously, ranging from high-pressure work with considerable demands and responsibility, to what are conversationally referred to as 'gofer' jobs (as in 'Go for some coffee/a newspaper', etc). Even these latter seemingly pointless activities may on occasion, if the office in question is important in the organization's running, offer the chance of establishing ties and connections with influential figures in it who may be of service in finding a position at a later date. The communications industries vary somewhat in this respect, but there is no question that such interpersonal networks are the main way the job market works in Hollywood, in particular, and in the broadcast and cable industries to a very large extent as well. Formal advertisements of job-openings are generally a secondary, almost emergency reserve method of recruitment.

All in all, however, internships are probably the single most important avenue to a communications career. They frequently enable young people to get a realistic sense of the timbre of working life in the given industry, and sometimes will provide direct access to the organization within which they have worked, once they have graduated. This means that gaining access to internships is, even if not a *sine qua non*, none the less a central route to the acquisition of a communications career by members of ethnic minority groups. In turn, the department's internship organizer represents a key figure in the process: she/he it is who will make many of the connections with employers, who will verify – or fail to – that valuable experience is likely to be gained by the student, and who in the case of ethnic minority students is in a position to be either supportive or unhelpful.

College and university programmes in communications have become very common and extremely well populated with students over the past decade. Again, they vary tremendously in content and quality. A key question in all of them, not least for our purposes here, consists in their relation to communication careers. Some heavily emphasize strictly academic content, in the traditional sense of lectures, seminars, essays and studies, sometimes offering master's and doctoral programmes. Others more nearly approach the model of a trade training school, with very considerable exposure to practical media activities, whether in the studio, in marketing exercises, in professional writing or elsewhere. Access to studio-based courses and computer terminal-based courses is typically highly competitive, with many students unable to gain access to them because of the limited number of places. One result is that a significant proportion of communication students in the United States currently graduate with a major in some aspect of media, but without significant practical training: for them, the degree is roughly equivalent to an English or sociology degree a few years earlier in the century.

The strongly practical format is most characteristic of the junior college/community college sector (colleges of further education in the United Kingdom) where there is generally an attempt to find what the industry is looking for in its entry-level recruits, and then to supply that training. Graduates of these two-year programmes are usually relatively successful in finding entry-level positions after graduation, but with only a two-year diploma, upward movement within their careers is often rather tightly bounded. Paradoxically, graduates from the more traditionally academic pro-grammes sometimes find it harder to gain entry-level positions, partly because their immediate supervisors may have joined the industry before a college degree was expected, and partly because their training has been less specific. None the less, their longer term prospects are definitely superior in general to those of community college graduates.

A further issue with a direct bearing upon ethnic minority groups, partially mediated by social class vectors as well, is the recruitment pattern of universities as opposed to that of community colleges. While there are a number of the latter located in affluent professional areas, and with excellent facilities, the tendency is strong for members of working class communities, if they attend courses after high school at all, to go to community colleges and, in such cases, often to institutions with poor funding and facilities. Dedicated instructors may compensate in part for these deficiencies, but they cannot transform a two-year diploma into a four-year degree. Furthermore, although the official Federal education policy concerning community colleges has been that they should constitute in part a way-station to degree-level study, in practice that way-station has rarely been utilized, and when it has, com-munity college graduates have frequently found the transfer very alienating, unset-tling and unconducive to their advance. The drop-out rate for transferring students is rather high.

Insofar, then, as members of ethnic minority groups in the United States are more often than not also members of the working class (not, be it noted, of 'the poor', that convenient abstraction in American public discourse on economic inequality), this community college/four-year-institution division is of considerable significance to ethnic minorities, especially as regards career prospects. And communications careers are no exception to this rule. Again, there are no statistics available currently to document this observation, but it is one with which few people familiar with American post-secondary education would take issue.

College newspapers, radio, television and cable stations, as noted above, may also offer important professional experience to students. Like their parent institu-tions, there is tremendous variety in quality and frequency, with some newspapers such as *The Daily Texan* (University of Texas, Austin) employing one hundred and forty people, and others using the services of two or three persons and appearing intermittently. None the less, many employers look for evidence of experience in student media, and thus they too constitute part of the potential avenue to a media career for ethnic minority group members.

Finally, there is the ethnic minority sector of the United States communica-tions industry (see Downing, 1988b, for references). As in other nations, this is a very fast-changing and under-researched sector. Indeed, while many ethnic minority media have in the past typically been underfunded and have often had to struggle for survival, since the late 1980s there has been an expansion in financially profitable

East Asian media, especially on the West Coast of the United States. These media have in no meaningful respect emerged from the experience of racial discrimination or oppression, the typical pattern for their counterparts up until then.

Probably the most significant ethnic minority sector in terms of numbers and market penetration is constituted by the Spanish-language broadcast and print media (Downing, 1992; Subervi-Vélez, 1986, 1987). However, with the huge wave of immigration into the United States during the 1980s from South East Asia and Latin America, not only do newspapers and magazines in the languages of all the nationalities concerned proliferate, but there are also more and more rented time-slots in television and radio programming. KSCI 18 in Los Angeles, about which more is noted below, is only the leading example of a national phenomenon. Admittedly these slots are sometimes filled with programme exports from the nation in question, but often there is programming produced domestically in the United States as well, and then sometimes syndicated across the country. Some of the most imaginative and creative video-making in the country, in absolute terms, and not just by comparison with American television fare, is emerging from Asian-American circles. The high penetration of cable television and its interface with satellite communications also offers the technical means for more diverse programming, and thus more scope to ethnic minority groups. Unfortunately this does not signify actual, as opposed to potential, widespread access, at least as yet. This is not least because multi-channel cable systems (i.e. those with more than twelve channels) are still often absent in multi-ethnic areas of large cities, and in scattered rural communities and reservations where a proportion of Native Americans reside.

In turn, a number of people make a transition from these media to mainstream ones, developing their careers in that direction. Some continue to operate in both. A different kind of example again is offered by the *Lakota Times*, noted below, where the preference of the staff is to stay with the paper on the grounds that they find it a more congenial workplace than major media newsrooms.

These then are the main sources of training for, and access to, professional media careers for members of such groups in the United States. (The further or, in career terms, later question of career development for ethnic minorities within a media organization (see Pease & Stempel, 1990) is also important but outside our present scope.) Let us now turn to some specific examples and experiences of how these training opportunities have worked.

Examples

I must comment initially on the very considerable difficulty encountered in gathering detailed data in this area, not least representative data (which the cases below make no claim to being). Despite the writer's seemingly favourable position as head of one of the leading university programmes in media education in the country, endless telephone calls to media institutions across the country drew blank after blank, with some people reluctant to return calls, others unwilling to share information, and still others eventually telling the researcher that the information was not available. In some instances, intelligence shared with the researcher that particular programmes existed to assist members of ethnic minority groups turned out to be unfounded.

One instance in particular struck the researcher, namely his failure to elicit information from CNN in Atlanta, Georgia. The links between his institution and CNN are really quite close, and yet the official in the CNN Personnel Department pronounced herself unable to say whether or not any interns in recent times had come from ethnic minority groups. Her support for this statement was based on the claim that records were not kept to identify interns by ethnic group status. All of which may be perfectly true, but it seemed distinctly odd that in Atlanta, a city with a very large African-American population, her own eyesight could not have led her to recall any Black interns. In the context of the assault on civil rights referred to above, the researcher was inevitably led to feel sceptical that the whole story was being told him. And, in turn, to wonder whether some of the blind alleys encountered elsewhere in the investigation, in terms of calls repeatedly not returned, did not reflect the same underlying issue.

A further research difficulty consisted in locating former interns once they had moved on. Unless they kept in touch with their former supervisors, which in turn would tend to select those whose internship experiences were very favourable, there was no obvious means of tracking them down. Thus the dimension of the research assignment which requested for experiential material proved to be rather hard, though not impossible, to supply.

The institutions and programmes to be commented upon are the following: Asian Cinevision, New York City; Black Entertainment Television, Washington DC; KSCI TV station, Los Angeles; the *Lakota Times*, Rapid City, South Dakota; Univision, New York City; the University of Southern California's Communications Management Master's Degree programme, Los Angeles; and Young & Rubicam's internship programme in New York City. The strong representation of New York City and Los Angeles is appropriate, given both their status as the two largest cities in the United States and the prominence of the communications industry there. It will also be evident that ethnic minority institutions in fact predominate, being much more forthcoming on this issue than the major communications institutions. This may, again, reflect that growing official disinterest in ethnic minority rights on the part of the ethnic majority to which reference has already been made.

The only major employer in the list is Young & Rubicam, although in fairness it is appropriate to note that the researcher did not attempt to gather data from the three major broadcast networks, or from the major studios in Hollywood. However, the decision not to do so was based upon a prior sense of the difficulty, without the possibility of personal interviews with the personnel departments involved, of assessing the public relations material which would inevitably be the response from a larger organization to questions about ethnic minority affairs. An example of this problem, drawn from Howard Wachtel's research and cited in Downing (1988a), is the habit of the networks to neglect the particular status of their New York City operations in trumpeting their equal opportunity policies, when the proportion of ethnic minorities in those key executive offices is exceptionally low.

All the four major categories of ethnic group utilized in American public discourse are touched upon, namely African-Americans, Hispanic Americans, Native Americans and Asian-Americans. The term 'Asian-American' represents an instance of a common feature of racial discourses, namely extraordinary imprecision. The largest Asian-American group consists of Americans of Filipino origin and not, as is conventionally perceived, Chinese; furthermore, over the decade of the 1980s, there was a considerable infusion of new migrants from South Asia. In other words, the category covers a very great variety of cultures and class differences. It is used here with that caveat.

There is a certain bias toward television and film in the institutions under review, and no representation at all of the public relations industry. Telecommunications management is touched upon in the case of one graduate of the Media Management programme at the University of Southern California. It is hoped none the less that the following observations will raise useful questions for more detailed investigation in future.

Asian Cinevision (ACV, New York City)

Founded in 1977, Asian Cinevision has functioned on a variety of levels over the years since. It has organized an annual Asian and Asian-American Film and Video Festival, has given advice and network support to numerous Asian-American filmmakers, some of whom are now making a major name for themselves in the United States and elsewhere, and has given a number of Asian-Americans the opportunity to learn media skills. It has also mounted a weekly cable television programme in New York City, and was one of the very first such projects. And not least, during the years it has operated, it has organized training workshops in video production, given people working with it a variety of experiences of the practical world of visual media, whether in exhibition or production, and acted as an employment conduit to many individuals, thus enabling them to begin professional media careers. In these ways, although not a large organization, it is one of the most interesting and effective ethnic minority media institutions in the film and video world in the United States.

One person who passed through this route on her way to her current career with CBS Television's International Advertising and Cable Sales department spoke of her professional media experiences in relation to Asian Cinevision. Her initial media experience was in journalism school at the Chinese University of Hong Kong followed by three years as a scriptwriter for the main Hong Kong television station. Despite this experience, she found herself frequently intimidated as a woman in the rather macho film community in Hong Kong and, when she migrated to New York City in 1980, decided to do less demanding and exhausting work than had been the case in Hong Kong television. She became involved with the Chinatown History Project, a progressive group of young Chinese who sought both to uncover the true history of New York's Chinatown, and to participate in labour and community issues in the present.

Her ambition to work less intensively was soon defeated. She found herself, to her delight, working on sound, camera and all aspects of video in the various media activities of the Chinatown History Project which worked fairly closely with Asian Cinevision. During that time her connections with Asian Cinevision were principally through the History Project. In 1987 and 1991, however, she helped coordinate and curate two screen festivals for ACV. She also co-produced a film entitled *Freckled Rice*.

In 1986 she began working freelance for CBS International on the business side, focusing on television exchanges between China and the United States. Both her media experience and bilingual skills were important in getting her the job. Some years later, the job was made permanent. Currently she is involved both in barter trade with the People's Republic of China, and in selling CBS programmes to Chinese-language cable operations in the United States.

Her experience in her current job has been positive, in that she is surrounded by people with similar language skills and international experience. In other words, the experience of many ethnic minority group members, of being the only such person in the newsroom or the studio, has not been hers. Looking back over her career to date, she feels she has experienced more problems as an Asian woman than as an Asian *per se*. She would like to be involved again in production and recognizes that she is occupying a particular, rather finely defined occupational niche, but her experience none the less has been a positive one in most respects.

Black Entertainment Television (BET)

This is a cable company located in Washington DC and the brainchild in very large part of Robert Johnson, its Chief Executive. Its corporate affiliation is with one of the giant Multiple System Operators of the American cable industry, Telecommunications Inc. In full operation since 1987, its programmes are carried nationwide.

BET takes five to eight interns each year in its Public Relations division and its Marketing and Sales division. They are drawn from a group of universities in the Washington metropolitan region, and usually spend four hours a day, two or three days a week, over the period of one semester, or over the summer vacation. The internships are not paid. They begin with a special orientation session, after which each intern is assigned to a particular set of tasks. For example, in the Public Relations division, they focus on such matters as press releases, on research identifying the best station for publicity purposes in a particular TV market area, on finding still photographs from record companies for publicity purposes, or on rate card research on the competitors in a given TV market.

The Director of Special Market Development to whom the researcher spoke said that the interns had always appeared to have tremendously high motivation. Occasionally when filing, this impetus might be seen to flag a little, but provided that explanation was forthcoming of how crucial good files were to an efficient organization, and about how much could be learned about an organization through an understanding of its filing system, the matter was usually resolved soon enough. This stands as an illustration of a more general function of such training, namely education in the daily matter-of-fact practicalities of professional performance. Few people know of these issues by instinct alone, and this kind of basic information, for a young man or woman without professional experience in their family, is both essential and – when absent – disastrous for employment prospects. Due to centuries of discrimination at all levels, the proportion of members of ethnic minorities without this kind of employment experience in their families is still quite high.

No interns had ever been taken on permanently in BET, in part at least because they were always having to finish their university studies before seeking full-time employment. Only one or two interns employed by the organization had not been people of colour.

One woman who had done two internships at BET, and between these a further public relations internship at a Black public relations firm in Hollywood, described the experience as extremely positive in all three cases. In the competitive world of the 1990s, she argued that a minimum of three internships was necessary for someone seeking a media career after graduation. Far more knowledge had come her way through those positions than in the classroom, not least the experience of having to learn to write well and to do so quickly at a moment's notice. The opportunity to make contacts and, as she put it, assemble a reference library of people to call later when in search of a position, had been invaluable. Ninety per cent of her peers told her they had gained their positions through contacts rather than through job-advertisements. Working in a small firm (her experience in Hollywood) had been very informative in the sense that she had to acquaint herself with all aspects of the work. Working in Black firms had, by comparison with the experience of some of her peers, offered her a support system not available in White corporations where, again in her own words, you often begin with a strike against you even before you walk through the door.

KSCI TV *(Los Angeles)*

KSCI has been in operation since 1988. It is a multi-lingual station, communicating especially though not exclusively to Asian publics in the Los Angeles and San Diego areas (the latter through a special booster transmitter). The languages include Arabic, Armenian, Cantonese, Hebrew, Hindi, Italian, Japanese, Khmer, Korean, Mandarin Chinese, Spanish, Tagalog, Thai and Vietnamese. Some of these audiences are very affluent, especially the Japanese and Korean sectors. Thus as well as being a fascinating television experiment in cultural terms, KSCI is also financially solvent.

The station does not take many interns a year – only three per university semester – but is actively committed to its internship programme. Its policy is to try to have the range of faces on its staff that are also on the screen, and this applies to its interns as well. It prefers people with some international experience, such as may be obtained in the United States Peace Corps, rather than necessarily people having one of the languages in which the station broadcasts.

Often the interns in KSCI will be assigned to the research department, though ultimately they are oriented through need rather than any other factor. Usually interns do not return to work in the station afterwards. Some return to work in the nation from which they originated. Only one, with particular statistical skills, had been hired part-time by the station. From the perspective of the station manager, the station offers an unusual experience to its staff who are enabled and encouraged to retain their ethnic and cultural identities. None the less KSCI constitutes a professional mainstream media outlet, and in that sense is not 'ethnic' or 'community' in character.

The Lakota Times (Rapid City, South Dakota)

In operation since 1979, the *Lakota Times* is a weekly newspaper based in the 60,000-strong town of Rapid City. Of that number, 8,000 are Native Americans. The editor of the paper, who also founded it, defines the project he has brought to life and sustained over the years as a more successful model for Native American media than many others, principally because it is commercially solvent and relies entirely on its own resources. Other Native American newspapers and radio stations generally rely for funding upon grants and donations, with their attendant vagaries and uncertainties, and with the dependence that they often entail. Many are owned by tribal governments, which frequently makes it hard for them to criticize the latter. With twenty employees in all, the paper is the largest private employer of Native Americans in the city.

Journalistic routines and practices have not been common among Native Americans, one significant reason being that the First Amendment was not held to apply to Indian nations, since these were defined as wards of the United States Government to be administered by the Bureau of Indian Affairs. The historical tendency has been for Native American journalists to privilege speaking out about their situation over reporting it (including reporting of important internal disagreements where they existed).

In this context, and in the context of the often dreadful economic situation of Native Americans, suffering from exceptionally high unemployment and poor educational attainment, the chief editor considers that his newspaper has played an important role. He points to his present editor as one example, a man who in 1979 was working for the newspaper as janitor, but who has learned his professional skills by working his way up the levels of competence inside the paper. The stability of staff on the paper has been high, except in the earliest years when some individuals were tempted to move on to other newspapers because of the initially low salaries paid at the *Lakota Times*. But since then, hardly anyone has chosen to leave.

The chief editor puts this down to the fact that working in his newspaper offers a far more sympathetic environment than working in a mainstream newspaper. To work in one of those, he argues, changes the person; an individual person cannot alter the newspaper. In his perspective, only urbanized Indians who have largely lost their culture would be likely to be at ease and to function well in such a setting. At the same time, he is insistent on his thoroughgoing editorial commitment to offer the most objective reporting possible in his newspaper. In his view, in no way does this mean training Native American journalists to be schizophrenics, any more than for any other journalists. Looking at reality through the eyes of Native Americans will add a necessary perspective to reporting, he argues, but it equally means offering a service to readers to make their own decisions about how to evaluate events, not to seek to pre-empt that process for them.

This case presents some interestingly different issues from some of the others, in that there is no wish, rather the reverse, to have people join mainstream media; yet at the same time, there is a commitment to operate according to the best standards of mainstream media, and in the process to educate a whole new group of people in the practice of journalism; and yet in that process, not to lose their Native identity and perspective.

Univision (New York City)

Based in New York City and Miami, Florida, Univision is the former Spanish International Network which in 1986 was judicially determined to contravene United States laws against media by being owned more than 50 per cent by non-nationals (in this case, Mexican nationals). Its owners sold the network to Hallmark Cards, the current owners. As of 1991, it was the main Spanish-language TV network in the country.

The internship programme operated by Univision focused mainly (70 per cent) on high school students, as opposed to the other programmes under review here, which drew mostly on college students. Univision worked with a general internship programme entitled 'I Have A Dream', sponsored by Colgate-Palmolive, and recruited high school students through that means. The network also worked with a second programme called 'Summerjobs', which brought in a few more. The two programmes had been in operation since 1987, and over the subsequent four years had up to fifteen interns working in Univision in New York. (Other programmes were in operation in Miami, but were not investigated.) The programme operated over the months of June to August, and gave each young person a specific set of tasks to perform, as well as inculcating business standards of dress, punctuality and responsibility. But they were not used as 'gofers', and indeed were often given computer training in the course of their internship. Comment was made on their high motivation, and on the way that, although three days a week were all that was required of them by way of attendance, many would put in extra hours in order to complete an assignment on time.

Over and above the utilization of high school students, some other people had made individual applications for internships. Of those, a couple of interns who were beyond college age had been taken on full time in the organization. The majority of applicants were Spanish-speaking, signifying that almost all were of Hispanic American origin.

Communications Management MA *(University of Southern California)*

As already argued above, careers on the business side of the communications industries are as important to consider in the context of this research project as are any of the more familiar and visible (i.e. glamorous) roles. The large Communications Management MA programme at the Annenberg School of Communication in the University of Southern California (USC) in Los Angeles has been in existence now for ten years. Overall, at any one time, there are perhaps a hundred or more students in the programme. There are no data available for the percentage of ethnic minority students who have graduated from the programme, but the internship coordinator was able to give me the names of five students for whom she had addresses. For Southern California, graduation from this programme is definitely a major gateway to a media career, and media institutions in other parts of the nation also employ quite a number of its graduates. USC is a private and expensive university to attend, although there are scholarships of which some students can avail themselves which take care of tuition and other fees.

One graduate with whom I was able to speak has been working as manager of a teleconferencing centre since 1989, having graduated that summer from the programme. Her view of the programme was that it was well organized, but set at a level relevant to much later stages in a communications industry career. She felt it would be years before she would be in a position to make use of much of the information and many of the ideas to which she had been exposed. She also observed that she was in an unusually favourable working environment in terms of having to deal with ethnic prejudice among her co-workers. The nature of her job meant that she worked largely on her own with clients. So long as they were happy, her employers were happy. Her fellow-employees were themselves of varying ethnic backgrounds, and the owner of the teleconferencing centre, employing only about ten people in all, was an Orthodox Jew, which she felt to have positive consequences for the atmosphere in the firm. Problems she had previously had as a Hispanic American in other jobs had not surfaced at all in this one, although she fully expected that when she made her next career move, they would be almost certain to face her wherever she went. She commented, interestingly in view of the Asian-American media worker's experience cited earlier, that so far she had had more problems professionally due to her gender, than to her ethnic status. A similar response emerged from some respondents to a survey of forty-two ethnic minority newspaper executives (Pease and Stempel, 1990, p. 70).

Young and Rubicam, Inc. *(New York City)*

The firm has two internship programmes, one informal, the other formal. Informally, students from colleges in the city work unpaid for three days a week at least, generally in management rather than on the creative side. The initial connection and every other feature of the arrangement depends entirely on the individuals concerned. If a position opens up in that area, such interns stand a good chance of being taken on as paid employees. By the nature of the operation, statistics are not kept, so that it is impossible to know whether or how many members of ethnic minority groups have benefited from the practice.

The other programme has been in existence since 1983, and is very carefully organized, with weekly seminars and a formal evaluation at the end of the programme. In 1991 there were seven hundred applications for just fifteen places (although in the stronger economy of the previous year there had been twice as many places). Each successful candidate is paid to work full-time for ten weeks over the summer. Applicants must be undergraduates in the second half of their third year of study, or the first half of their final year, to qualify. The programme is organized to try to select not only the highly talented, but also to ensure a strong representation of ethnic minorities. The organizers work closely with the Minority Internship Programme of the American Association of Advertising Agencies, also based in New York City. In 1991, out of the fifteen successful candidates, four were from ethnic minority groups, and were placed one each in the departments of Art, Accounts Management, Media and Research.

The process of selection is a hard one, not least because a surprising number of applicants already have some or even considerable experience in the industry. This reality is important to bear in mind, because typically they will have achieved this experience not only through native talent but also through connections in advertising firms. For members of ethnic minority groups, seriously under-represented in the industry, such connections are likely to be missing.

With such a large applicant pool, about eighty of whom are interviewed personally, there is little impetus to go out and visit colleges, although some such visits are made each year. The internships tend to focus on the management side of the industry, simply because the creative aspect of the process is exceptionally hard to inculcate via a formal placement. Finally, as in other programmes, the later career experience of interns is hard to ascertain unless they keep in touch. Very often, even a success story only becomes known as a result of a chance encounter with a former intern.

Concluding comments

Significant as these various avenues are for professional media careers, it is difficult to begin to get a handle on the exact extent to which they have served members of ethnic minority groups. Statistics are generally not kept, knowledge of the later careers of interns is often absent, the work-experiences of such individuals have not been widely recorded, and thus the overall picture remains fuzzy. None the less, if there is one conclusion that may be drawn, it is that the presence or absence of members of ethnic minority groups in all echelons of the communications industry is not only vital in terms of employment justice, and is not only crucial in terms of non-racist and anti-racist media representation and discourse, but is practically speaking *pivotal* to the proper future employment of members of ethnic minority groups because of the networking character of finding employment in most if not all sections of the industry. Especially, but far from exclusively, at executive levels. And even more intensively so during economic recession.

References

Bushnell, V. (1990): Few Blacks and Hispanics in Agencies, Reports of Racism and Hostility Cited. *Back Stage*, 11 May, pp. 1, 50–51.

Downing, J.D.H. (1988a): Media employment of Blacks in the United States. In: J. Harte, (ed.). *Black People and the Media*. United Kingdom, Warwick University Publications, pp. 93–109.

Downing, J.D.H. (1988b): Ethnic minority radio in the United States. *Howard Journal of Communication*, 2.2, pp. 135–148.

Downing, J.D.H. (1992): Spanish-language media in Greater New York. In: S. Riggins (ed.). *Ethnic minority media: an international perspective*. California, Newbury Park, Sage Publications.

Gilliam, D.B. (1991): Harnessing the assets of a multicultural future. *Media Studies Journal*, 5.4, Fall, pp. 127–135.

Kern-Foxworth, M. (1989a): Status and roles of minority public relations practitioners. Public Relations Review, 15.3, Fall, pp. 39–47.

Kern-Foxworth, M. (1989b): Minorities 2000: the shape of things to come. *Public Relations Journal*, 45.8, August, pp. 14–22.

Pease, T. & Stempel G.H. III. (1990): Surviving to the top: views of minority newspaper executives. *Newspaper Research Journal*, 11.3, pp. 64–79.

Subervi-Vélez, F. (1986): The mass media and ethnic assimilation and pluralism. *Communication Research*, 13.1, pp. 71–96.

Subervi-Vélez, F. (1987): Toward an understanding of the role of the mass media in Latino political life. *Social Science Quarterly*, 68.1, pp. 185–196.

2

Ethnic minorities in the media: the case of the Netherlands

L.M. Bovenkerk-Teerink

Introduction

Why would well-established majorities share power and resources with insignificant minority groups? Are there any circumstances and conditions conceivable in which a 'host' society grants influence and power to immigrant communities? All immigration countries have to face this question and the answer is usually negative. The same holds for post-war Western Europe where there can be no doubt that majority peoples favour the assimilation of individual immigrants rather than giving them rights as ethnic groups. The general view has been that such group rights make for the kind of pluralism that threatens the political stability of the state.

In this paper I want to describe how a Northern-European-type welfare state, the Netherlands, offers a rare historical instance in which group integration has been promoted through sharing with immigrants in the central institutions of society. The institution in question is the national Dutch radio and television broadcasting system. I intend to show that although the attempt has been fraught with unforeseen complications, and has never been more than a paternalistic policy – with favours being extended rather than rights granted – a modest success has nevertheless been achieved. State intervention has been absolutely crucial to the development of a media policy for ethnic minorities and the paper therefore surveys at some length the various government documents.

Which immigrant groups form the Dutch ethnic minorities?

The Netherlands has one of Europe's smallest minority populations. Only Denmark has less (3 per cent of its inhabitants) and Britain equals the Netherlands with 6 per cent. Other West European countries have more than 9 per cent. The Netherlands therefore stands apart for its diversity. It has citizens who themselves or their parents originate from: (a) former colonies, e.g. Indonesia, the Netherlands Antilles and Aruba, Surinam; (b) Mediterranean countries such as Greece, Italy, Morocco, Portugal, Spain, Tunisia, Turkey and the former Socialist Federal Republic of Yugoslavia; (c) Chile, the former Czech and Slovak Federal Republics, Vietnam and other countries that have produced refugees, and (d) a miscellaneous group hailing from the Cape Verde Islands, China and the Philippines. A large group of Eurasian refugees from Indonesia (300,000) are not considered as constituting an ethnic minority because they are considered to be assimilated and to not show a social profile of ethnic disadvantage.

The state has defined who the minorities are, perhaps more so than any other Western European country. Moluccans (40,000) originating from East Indonesia, Surinamese (220,000), Antillians (40,000, including immigrants from the Island of Aruba) and Mediterranean groups (400,000) have been selected by the government as target groups for its social minority policy. The state has created a complex system of help and assistance for these ethnic minorities and almost certainly spends a lot more money on help per head than any other European country. Although the Netherlands has often been used as a positive reference country in this respect, it by no means implies that minorities have equal access to jobs, housing and other social amenities. In fact, some groups suffer from extremely high rates of unemployment, many as much as 50 per cent. Minorities are still grossly under-represented in positions of political power. Their small number and enormous ethnic variation has contributed to their being perceived as groups in need of help by the caring state rather than as a factor of political importance. Contrary to other European countries where immigrants have been considered a threat and minorities as 'an enemy within', minorities in the Netherlands have been turned into objects of paternalistic benevolence and peoples dependent on the state.

The Dutch broadcasting system

The Dutch have an amazingly complex system of media organization that is neither state-controlled nor commercial. Its complexity has to be attributed to the specific Dutch historical event of harmony between ten various denominational 'pillars' of society. Each pillar used to have its own broadcasting association, one Catholic, two Protestant and one Social-Democrat, which were the largest. The system is based on mutual tolerance, non-intervention and individual sovereignty (Lijphart, 1968). Content is determined by broadcasting organizations, with the state playing an institutional regulatory role only. The *Mediawet* (media statute) sets the rules for recognizing such associations, allocates broadcasting time, protects freedom of opinion and guarantees diversity of opinion via broadcasts and the press. In accordance with liberal practices, Dutch broadcasting associations compete for time on the national networks. Two new associations that began in the 1970s have not been organized on the basis of denominational support. These are now the largest ones, thereby demonstrating the withering-away of the denominational pillar system. According to the *Mediawet*, an association is entitled to broadcasting time when it has at least 150,000 members who support the organization through payment of a contribution. Larger associations receive more broadcasting time than smaller ones. There are currently eight major broadcasting associations. Time and state-levied media consumers' tax is divided among these organizations on three television channels and five radio channels. In addition, there is one purely commercial television channel and several radio channels (see Reinsch, 1988).

The 'players'

The Minister of Welfare, Health and Culture is politically responsible for the implementation and safeguarding of the *Mediawet*. The Minister is advised by a media council (mediaraad).

The *Nederlandse omroepstichting* (NOS), or national broadcasting system, is the body that coordinates the distribution of broadcasting time among the various associations. In addition it produces joint programmes that meet the social and cultural needs of (smaller) audiences, when these are not met by the separate associations. NOS has a *Programmaraad* (programme council) that counts at least one representative of ethnic minorities among its members. Actually there are now two of these.

The *Stichting Omroep Allochtonen* (STOA), or ethnic minorities' broadcasting foundation, represents joint minority media interests. It is a pressure group that has been accepted as an advisory body by the Ministry of Welfare, Health and Culture since 1986.

Dutch minority policy after 1980

The Netherlands had a fully-fledged social policy for ethnic minorities between 1980 and 1989, and this period is the main subject of this chapter. In 1989 a fundamental change in this policy was announced, although it has hardly been implemented to date. The latest development will be dealt with at the end of the chapter.

1980–1989

The many different names that have been attributed to the newcomers clearly reflect the varying ways in which the Dutch Government has defined its social and economic position. As in most European countries, they were regarded as 'migrants', 'foreign workers' and 'guest workers' at first. These three terms conveyed the idea that their stay would be short. In fact nobody, including the immigrants themselves, thought of permanent settlement. This changed in the course of the 1970s. Immigrants from former colonies (Indonesia, Surinam, the Netherlands Antilles) stayed for good and had the right to do so as they were Netherlands citizens. Those who had arrived as migratory labourers were granted the right to family reunion and a majority of these single men seized the opportunity. The acknowledgement that the immigrants would stay permanently cannot by itself be considered sufficient cause for the development of a comprehensive ethnic minority policy that sets the Dutch case somewhat apart from other European countries. The dramatic events of Young Molucca terrorism in the mid-1970s (including hijacking of trains) changed the nature of the situation completely. Although the hijackers themselves claimed a political objective (the realization of the independent Republic of the Free Moluccas), the Dutch authorities regarded it as the outward expression of a second-generation immigrants' problem. There was a strong feeling that other groups would cause similar problems if their needs were not attended to, and that immigrant groups could easily become unintegrated groups in society and thereby threaten the social order. Consequently it was felt that without a minority policy, the next generation of immigrants might prove to be the 'social time-bomb' that so many Europeans have been afraid of. Accordingly, Dutch minority policy originated not from a conception of social justice, but rather from a concern for political containment. Nevertheless, Dutch minority policy has resulted in a set of programmes whose progressive nature has hardly been matched by other governments.

The time was ripe for an original approach. At the end of the 1970s, the Dutch believed that they would deal with the problem better than anyone else, with values central to Dutch cultural life such as tolerance and solidarity being manifest in this new minority policy. Cultural relativism became the paramount philosophical concept, and the caring state the instrument of social equality. The Netherlands Government's think-tank, the WRR (Netherlands Scientific Council for Government Policy), produced the main advisory paper in 1979. The title of the report proposed a new name for the groups in question: *ethnic minorities*. The Dutch would agree to let the immigrants stay for good, the old terminology implying differences was abandoned and the new ethnic minority group concept adopted. By accepting the report's analysis and policy recommendations, the Netherlands declared itself to be a multicultural society. At the time few people had given this concept of multiculturalism very much thought; the nation was broadly defined as a type of society in which different groups would live peacefully together and where each would adhere to its own culture in so far as it wished to do so; it would be a type of society in which groups would tolerate each other's uniqueness, with no one group dominating or suppressing another. Sociologically naive, the mere fact that the White indigenous society was very large indeed and that it held all means of power in its grasp, while minority groups were small and dispersed, was given little consideration.

Unlike other European countries the birth of a minority policy has been accompanied by a tremendous, and largely government-funded, scientific research endeavour. This also contributed to the conviction that the policy would prove a success. Individual researchers were brought together, projects were initiated and the government took over by organizing scientific production. An advisory body specifically for research on minorities (ACOM) was founded in 1979. The end result was that most research turned out to be of a descriptive and factual nature and 'ethnic minorities' were studied merely in terms of disadvantages which were supposed to characterize them. But all this is mere hindsight: at the time the mood was one of outspoken optimism.

The Minister of Home Affairs was given responsibity for the new Minorities policy and the job of coordinating other ministries' efforts in this respect. All government departments were entrusted with a task. A Minorities Policy Unit was set up as part of the Ministry of Home Affairs in 1979. The ethnic minority concept was redefined for day-to-day political practice by defining the groups in question as suffering from social deprivation and disadvantage. Social equality would be attained by first identifying factors that hinder social advancement and then designing a relevant remedy. Discrimination and racism were explicitly mentioned as possible causes of disadvantage.

The policy launched

Dutch minority policy was officially launched in 1983. It was based on the Government's paper on *Minderhedenbeleid* (Social policy for minorities) and its contents clearly echoed the extensive and daring propositions of the WRR-Report of four years before. The main objective was formulated as follows: 'The establishment of a society in which members of minority groups residing within the Netherlands acquire a social position of equality and experience full opportunities for development, both on an individual basis and as a group. 'The conceptual vehicle for equal opportunities was to be 'emancipation'. This term harks back to Dutch social history of the late nineteenth and early twentieth centuries when various religious denominations as well as the working class overcame their social and economic disadvantages and gained equality before the law by successfully fighting discrimination.

The Ministry targeted a wide range of minority groups for its policy: Antillians, Cape Verdeans, Italians, Moluccans, Moroccans, Portuguese, Spaniards, Surinamese, Turks and Yugoslavs as well as gypsies and caravan dwellers. For more than four generations the latter have comprised an indigenous group that is socially disadvantaged. Its inclusion demonstrated that the Dutch Government was determined to solve every single problem of persistent social deprivation. A little more than 4 per cent of the population residing in the Netherlands were supposed to belong to the diverse category of ethnic minority groups. Many concrete measures of social policy were introduced in various areas such as education, housing, employment, culture and social welfare in the years that followed. The legal status of expatriates has been considerably improved and foreign residents now have the right to vote in local elections. This comprehensive effort conceived in an atmosphere of progressiveness, optimism and enthusiasm also set the stage for what happened to immigrants in the media.

The Government's 1983 policy paper on minorities explicitly deals with the role that the media should play in bringing about a multicultural society. Media such as TV and radio were given the role of being instrumental in both making minorities into citizens of Dutch society and life, and facilitating the development of their own cultures. The paper acknowledged that thus far too little information had been made available about society as a whole for the designated groups and that opportunities to enjoy their cultural lives had been too few.

The policy measures following from this aimed first of all to enable NOS to rearrange air-time in favour of this type of programme. Secondly, the *Programmaraad* (Programme Council) was to make one seat available for a representative member of ethnic minorities. Thirdly, the paper held that local broadcasting initiatives should be exceptionally suited for programmes for and by these groups; the Ministry for Welfare, Health and Culture therefore subsidized a number of experiments for a three-year period from 1984 to 1986 in Amsterdam, Rotterdam and three smaller administrative centres. After 1986 the government's subsidies were maintained in the four big cities, Amsterdam, Rotterdam, The Hague and Utrecht. NOS was urged to lend a helping hand by making available additional programmes, and to assist by organizing courses for minority members to produce and make their own minority programmes. The same Ministry started a special audio-visual studio ('Studio IM', i.e. Minorities' information) in 1980 to assist minority broadcasting in liaison with other local broadcasting corporations and paid its costs for a five-year period. Since special attention was paid to women in minority groups, the Ministry of Social Affairs and Employment recently established an agency (VEM) to promote the employment of minority women in the media. The project's aim was and still is to help such women to find their way into employment through vocational training, market orientation and intercession. It benefits from the cooperation of a sister enterprise at the local Hilversum labour exchange.

This short summary of concrete projects and measures for minority inclusion in the media may help to demonstrate the government's good will. Dutch minority policy was designed to solve a substantial number of problems at the same time. There was money and an open attitude. Every institution was set to play its role. The Dutch minority policy would be a combined effort of the central government, local authorities, constructive minority organizations and labour unions, and there would be scientific research to accompany the whole programme.

The policy in operation

Let us now turn to the question of how the concept of multicultural society was shaped by this specific minority policy. Each and every government agency was required to give concrete form to the abstract principles through a series of papers. Thus a paper was written on employment and another on housing while, in the same vein, NOS issued its document on 'Ethnic-cultural minorities in the Dutch broadcasting system'. This drew heavily on an earlier paper written by six minority organizations in the country under the title of '*Van zwartwit naar kleur*' (From black and white to colour) and on the results of a scientific survey undertaken by NOS itself on watching and listening habits among eight nationalities. The 1982 NOS document reiterates the idea of multiculturality and adheres to the central government's philosophy, yet fails to identify sufficient means to put the idea into action. This was virtually inevitable, in fact, as most institutions naturally responded with pleas for more money and manpower and in this particular case, more air time. The NOS paper also points to the importance of regional and local broadcasting systems as a multi-ethnic society finds greater expression in the areas and cities where minorities are concentrated. The very same points were found in a follow-up NOS paper of 1984, under the same title. What was new was that NOS now wanted to invite a minority representation to be appointed to their governing bodies and more full-time personnel with a minority background. The extension of air time on behalf of minorities materialized through the creation of a special fund for 'educational and instructive broadcasting' by the Ministry for Welfare, Health and Culture. In accordance with the outcome of the survey on consumer preferences, the content of minority programmes was changed from information only to include cultural and more diverse programming.

Minority organizations played their role first by producing the aforementioned paper *From black and white to colour*, and then by creating a special platform, i.e., STOA. It currently monitors what is happening in the media nationally, regionally and at the local level, comments on new developments and proposes policy measures. Its members regularly meet NOS and the Ministry concerned, inform LAO (i.e. the national advisory body of minority organizations), talk to civil servants at different administrative levels and organize conferences. By participating in the political structures and through its lobbying work, STOA tries systematically to keep minorities high on the media agenda. Since 1989 STOA has been continually funded by the government.

As far as labour unions are concerned, their modest contribution comprises the creation of a working group called 'Migrants and media'. This body is concerned with the images of minority groups as presented by the media and recently it has begun fighting for better legal status for ethnic employees in the press and the broadcasting system. The Christian labour union (CNV) has a prominent member of Turkish descent who mediates in negotiations between Dutch media employers and its ethnic group members.

Mention should also be made of the initiative of the schools of journalism that co-operate with and receive funding from the Ministry of Social Affairs and Employment to open regular courses to minorities. Their 1988 report *Aangeboden allochtone journalisten* (Allochtonous journalists 'for sale') contained a recommendation to fix a 5 per cent quota for minorities. That suggestion has been adopted and put into practice, although it is too early to evaluate the results.

Finally, we come to empirical scientific research. Almost all scientific work on minorities and the media in the Netherlands shows immediate policy concerns. In their comparative study of media usage among ethnic minorities in six European countries, Schakenbos and Marsman (1988) counted no less than 13 empirical reports in the Netherlands alone. Their study argues that such reports only show fragments, dealing with a few ethnic groups such as Moroccans and Turks and a few media such as radio and television, and that the main focus is on the time and frequency of media use rather than on what the minority audiences concerned would prefer. They also show that research interest in media usage closely corresponds to ideas in government circles, as well as within NOS, on what constitutes the minority problem that should be addressed by their policies. The present author quite agrees with this conclusion. The scientific yield after 1988 is not much different. It contains statements written by administrators, including rather superficial policy papers on functions, ideals and plans and some evaluations of the media. There is almost no contribution from psychologists or mass communication researchers and everything seems to have been dominated by policy makers and administrators. There is for example no tradition of research into the influence of the contents of media such as radio and television on the creation of stereotypes among the newcomers. We have only the report by Bovenkerk and Bovenkerk-Teerink on the creation of criminal stereotypes of Blacks in five national journals (1972); but this piece of work dates back to before the introduction of the Netherlands minority policy. There has also been the cumulative body of work on the written press by van Dijk (1983, 1991). The influence of radio and especially television must be far greater. This has created a paradoxical situation in which a country with readily available research funds and many excellent researchers does not take part in the international discussion on the subject. It is a case of governmental amnesia.

The results

To assess the results of this combined effort, I shall consider three of the media minority policy goals, as follows: (1) The extent to which ethnic minorities have been able to produce their own programmes; (2) The degree of access they have been granted to the overall national broadcasting system; (3)The final outcome of the ideas and intentions concerning local minority media initiatives.

Ethnic minority programmes

Prior to the introduction of the ethnic minorities media policy, there had been a few scattered programmes for immigrants on radio. As far back as 1960, VARA, the Social-Democratic political broadcasting organization, provided programmes of information for what were then called foreign workers. NOS took over and extended its audience by addressing other minority groups (Schakenbos & Marsman, 1988). This was to change with the introduction of the minority policy.

Schakenbos and Marsman (1988, pp. 68–69, 79–80) have made an inventory of national minority programmes that were being broadcast when the minority policy reached its zenith in 1987. It looks quite impressive. All the programmes mentioned were in the language of the country of origin, and all of them were made by members of the ethnic group themselves. They gave information about the current situation of the Netherlands and the country of origin and offered platforms for discussion within the immigrant communities. They operated in accordance with the 1975 Helsinki principle relating to 'the right for migrant workers to receive as far as possible regular information in their own language concerning both their country of origin and their host countries.'

According to the data of Schakenbos and Marsman, minority group members could see and listen to the following programmes:

Television

A. *Paspoort* (Passport), provided by NOS:

Italians	10 minutes per week
Moroccans	30 minutes per week
Spaniards	10 minutes per week
Turks	30 minutes per week
Yugoslavs	10 minutes per week

B. *Medelanders Nederlanders* (Co-patriots Netherlanders), provided by NOS;

44 hours per year for all ethnic minorities as a whole: Antillians, Cape Verdeans, Kurds, Moroccans, Portuguese, Spaniards, Surinamese, Turks, Yugoslavs and 'allochtonous youngsters'

C. *Islamidische Omroepstichting* (Islamic Broadcasting Foundation)

15 minutes per week

Languages spoken: Arabic, Dutch and Turkish

Radio

NOS provides:

Programmes of 30 minutes per week each in the language of the country of origin for Chinese, Greeks, Italians, Spaniards and Yugoslavs;

Programmes of 30 minutes per fortnight for Cape Verdeans and Portuguese;

Programmes of 10 minutes per day for Moroccans and Turks.

Nieuws voor buitenlanders (News for expatriates)

10 minutes per day per group for Moroccans in Moroccan Arabic and Berber, Spanish-speaking peoples and Turks

Tambu for Antillians

Suara Mauluku for Moluccans

Zorg en Hoop for Surinamese

All three 30 minutes or 45 minutes per week

Medelanders Nederlanders

60 minutes per week educational programmes for all minorities

Islamidsche Omroepstichting

1 hour per week in Arabic, Dutch and Turkish

Radio Thuisland (radio homeland)

1 hour per week for expatriate youngsters

Heber-ler, Kayen Ronja, OPODORO by Evangelical Broadcasting System

50 minutes per week for Moroccans, Surinamese and Turks.

While some might claim that this total looks quite impressive, it was necessarily diverse; and each separate group could rightfully claim that it was too little. It is noteworthy that such programmes were typically broadcast at odd hours and on channels of least importance. It has been pointed out that the typical programme for ethnic minorities went out on Netherlands radio channel 5 on Sunday night and in between programmes for other 'disadvantaged' minority groups such as homosexuals, handicapped persons and adherents of uncommon religions. At the present moment only the larger Moroccan and Turkish groups still retain their Paspoort television programmes. These have been transferred from a week-day to Sundays, which is regarded by the minorities as a degradation of their provision. Only half of the 105 hours per year are now specifically assigned to them; the other half, according to NOS, should address a broader audience than minorities alone. Such decisions were taken to dispose of the ghetto-like character of such programmes, and to give more attention to countries and cultures of origin rather than to the distressing aspects of the existence of minorities in the Netherlands. NOS claims that by so doing, the second generation of immigrants is being better served. One should realize that this is the result of proposals put by NOS very recently, and that it is hard to say therefore whether it will lead to more or less monoculturalism on the national television system. As we will see later, NOS policy has been to direct smaller groups to local television systems. Although the local systems have served these smaller groups for a few years, most major city systems have now decided in favour of the larger groups too.

Ethnic minority representation in the national broadcasting system

How many members of ethnic minorities have been employed by the big national and general broadcasting corporations? What levels do they work at? Do they work under the same conditions as their White Dutch colleagues? I have found it impossible to answer these questions definitely. Broadcasting associations refer to the laws on privacy and registration and claim they do not know. This may seem strange in a country that has a clear-cut minority policy and where many organizations claim to practise 'positive action'. Yet it should be remembered that the Netherlands were occupied during the Second World War, and that the Nazis were enabled to murder an unusually high percentage of Jews in the Netherlands precisely because

47

they were registered. Even when I know or suspect that the real reason for not giving numbers and facts on minorities is gross under-representation in the organization concerned, its management may successfully hide behind privacy considerations. The usual answer is: 'I cannot give any numbers because I don't know. I do not even want to know the ethnic background of my employees because I do not discriminate.'

However, through my own observation and interviews with people from such broadcasting associations, I feel certain that ethnic minorities are almost absent. The one example known to everybody in the Netherlands is a woman from Surinam who reads the daily news on TV. She has been hired for seven years for the explicit purpose of having somebody of colour for a change, and the director of the news programme openly stated that this was to be considered a major progressive move forward because ethnic minorities should now be visibly present in the system. She is still the only one in that position. The newly created commercial broadcasting corporation RTL4 has had the only Moroccan anchorman ever in its breakfast show. And VPRO, a small, liberal association, had a weekly migrants' talk show for about four years. The programme was discontinued because VPRO now claims that all of its programmes should show multicultural awareness. These very few cases are the only ones visible among many hundreds of TV people. All other visible minority employees are found in the typical and exclusive minority programmes listed above. They are what television personnel call the 'migrants' tape', and can be seen on TV-Channel 3 and heard on Radio Channel 5.

All of them work on a free-lance basis or with short-term contracts. This does not necessarily imply discrimination, as working on a short-term contract is quite common in the world of radio and television. Permanent editorial boards are typically small and it is not easy for anybody to obtain full-time employment. It is odd, to say the least, that none of the employees working for *Paspoort* or other branches of the 'migrants' tape' have been hired on a permanent basis. When measured by the yardstick of broadcasting associations themselves (as in their report '*Contractvormen*'), the position of minority employees is quite unacceptable. According to this report, freelancers should not be hired for prolonged, organizational work. Most collaborators of *Paspoort* have been working there for 10 to 15 years now. They work on the basis of 10-month contracts, which means that they have no income during the summer. They do not have the advantages of collective agreements and are in fact excluded from retirement programmes and unemployment benefit and may easily be laid off. The NOS point of view in the matter is that employees who have not fully mastered Dutch are confined to a limited range of tasks and cannot be regularly employed. Various organizations have tried to intervene on their behalf – among them the Netherlands Association of Journalists which has published two 'Zwartboeken' (résumés of the grievances of the minority personnel) on the matter – but so far without success.

This conflict clearly illustrates the problem. Ethnic minority people have been hired to work for the 'migrants' tape' only, and their specialization is held against them. This shows their marginal status. Although some of them do speak Dutch and have expressed their wish to be freed from working for 'the ethnic playground' only, they have not been successful so far. As one of them told me: 'Once *Paspoort*, always *Paspoort*'. This is clearly a case of ethnic mobility trapping (Wiley, 1967), and terms such as 'ethnic playground' refer to the existence of an ethnic ghetto within the Dutch broadcasting system. The people concerned are expected to be glad to be hired under the special minority policy. They were needed because they speak the language of the 'target group'.

One minority employee talks about himself as a 'language coolie' and feels that he has been hired for his ethnic background only, and not for any particular qualities as a broadcaster. The minority policy is proving to be a double-edged sword. Another interviewee in this category stated: 'In the beginning it is to your advantage that you belong to an ethnic group, but in the longer term it hinders your advancement'. The only way out seems to be to leave the minority ghetto completely behind. Some have taken the initiative to learn and speak Dutch to perfection – and they claim that the effort is tremendous since one has to be able to use Dutch twice as well as a native Dutchman if one is to be taken seriously; one has to follow all sorts of courses, and try to find a job outside the world of NOS and the broadcasting establishment. The second possibility is to found your own commercial enterprise, and some people have done just that. But it is not easy to compete with the many White Dutch firms that are now being created under the recent urge to commercialize. In fact the prospects for minority business people in this arena seem to be gloomy so far. Others do not seem to be aware of the trap they have run into and have been waiting for years for their employer to finally recognize their general skills. They have begged for the opportunity to follow the same staff development courses that their Dutch colleagues have been offered as part of good personnel policy, but so far in vain.

I have found only two men who have managed to stay out of the ghetto. One is the above-mentioned Moroccan reporter for the RTL4 commercial station. He is the exception that proves the rule because he was able to take special courses paid for by his employer. If he does not work for RTL4 any more, it is of his own free choice. The second one to be offered extra training works for the editorial board of the TV news programme. He is Black and claims that it will probably be many years before he is seen on the screen. Both feel that members of ethnic minorities do get a fair chance to work for regular programmes provided their Dutch is perfect, their education first class (preferably including the school for journalism) and, most telling and important of all, they are in no way whatsoever associated with the *Paspoort* ghetto. Being aware of network theory, they claim that having personal connections in the White male broadcasting circuit is essential.

This discussion of the position of individual minority members within the broadcasting system does not imply that special programmes for ethnic minority groups do not fulfil a relevant function. On the contrary, they draw large audiences and bridge something of the gap between the society of the White majority and the various ethnic minorities. Many minority reporters are dedicated to their work and feel they produce relevant information while providing the necessary amusement.

And, significantly, during the Gulf War a sizeable Dutch audience watched their programmes to obtain additional information and hear the Muslim point of view.

A final word should be said about the ethnic minorities' power to influence decision-making at the highest level. In accordance with the media statute, the *Programmaraad* (Programme Council) comprises at least one representative of ethnic minority groups. In fact, there are now two. One belongs to STOA and the other comes from the national minorities organization NCB (National Centre for Expatriates). Although the majority of this council is obviously White and Dutch, minority organizations apparently feel that their voice is being heard, because there are no complaints or conflicts. One should however realize that the peaceful co-operation of government-subsidized minority organizations characterizes the atmosphere of the whole multi-ethnic fabric in this country. Hence open conflict should be avoided in all political discourse in Dutch life, and this holds true for debates involving ethnic minorities and the media.

Local and regional broadcasting companies

The Netherlands now has 13 regional broadcasting structures and 228 local ones. These numbers are expected to rise. They perform a direct democratic function because all sorts of interest and pressure groups use them to voice their concerns. Twenty of these broadcast regularly on TV. Most regional structures have started through the initiative of volunteers, but the number of paid collaborators is increasing. Apart from national networks, none are subsidized by the national broadcasting fund. Regional and local companies rely on contributions from members, gifts, municipal support and donations from interest groups. They not only present journalistic products, but also carry out explicitly social and cultural functions. All parties agree, therefore, that local broadcasting systems can perform a crucial role in bringing about a multicultural society. Thus the Ministry for Welfare, Health and Culture decided to subsidize a number of experiments on a temporary basis with the assistance of NOS.

How far has the goal been attained? According to regulations for local broadcasting structures, a council exists representing all aspects of local society. Bastiaansen *et al.* (1990) have counted their numbers. Ethnic minority representation closely reflects their share in the local populations and communities. However, they do not seem to be included in executive management. The proportion of minority members employed in the regional and local structures is no more than 2.4 per cent. The groups represented are Moluccan, Moroccan, Turkish and Surinamese. About a third of all local companies have created slots for minorities, making an average of one in thirty-two air-hours available to them. Programmes have an informative and cultural content, with the largest groups being served in their own languages. Since all this is very recent, one might argue that something is indeed getting off the ground for minorities. The four big cities are out in front; they have immigrant broadcasting companies doing both radio and television. This started in Amsterdam and Rotterdam on the basis of a government subsidy in 1983, while The Hague and Utrecht joined only a few years ago.

MTV (Amsterdam)

MTV stands for Migrants' Television, a company created by the Ministry of Welfare, Health and Culture. Its aim is to further the participation of minorities in the media, to provide information in their own languages and, more generally, to see to it that the media reflect the social composition of the local population. They broadcast on the open channel of the local company *SALTO*. Although SALTO is ultimately responsible for its programme content, MTV is granted maximum leeway in practice. There are programmes for Antillians, Moroccans, Surinamese and Turks. Thursday is minority day, with each national or ethnic group being served once each month. MTV is free to decide on the allocation of air-time. Its funds come from the Ministry, the municipality of Amsterdam and its own sources. A special foundation has been created to train its personnel. Ten people work there full-time and 20 on a free-lance basis, and MTV has a number of volunteers. When plans materialize for a new commercial and professional channel, MTV will claim its share.

Mosaic (Rotterdam)

The Ministry's experiment has been less successful here than in Amsterdam. *Mosaic* has no say in the allocation of air time and the foundation has no representation in the local broadcasting structure. *Mosaic* goes out two hours per week (Sundays) on television on the open channel of the local broadcasting system of Rotterdam, and 43 hours per week on the radio. Their groups comprise Cape Verdeans, Greeks, Italians, Moroccans, Pakistanis, Surinamese, Turks and Yugoslavs. The Chinese have a programme on the radio only. Their sources of income are the same as in Amsterdam, which means that they are partly subsidized by the government and the community and partly through their own income from external productions. *Mosaic* would like to have greater influence. As there is no specific training centre for minority personnel, courses taken elsewhere have to be paid for.

MOS (The Hague)

MOS or Migrants' Broadcasting Foundation, started as an outcome of a project in 1985 to inform all expatriates living more than 5 years legally in the country of their voting rights in local municipal elections. It broadcasts on the open channel of the local broadcasting structure, LOKATEL. The executive board of MOS is represented on the LOKATEL council and helps to allocate air time. Since MOS is older and has equipment that LOKATEL does not have, tensions have risen between the two. LOKATEL itself has proven to be a competitor as it too makes programmes for minorities. There are programmes for Antillians and Surinamese combined and for Moroccans and Turks combined, and 8 minutes' programming per week for Chinese, Italians, Kurds, Pakistanis, Portuguese, Spaniards and Yugoslavs. More than in other cities, there is a conviction here that all groups, albeit small ones, should be addressed. Funds come from the Ministry and from the municipal authorities. MOS has set up its own training body for new personnel that tries to confine its relevance to The Hague only. Thus it hopes to avoid losing its trainees to other regional or even the national broadcasting structures. Training courses in Amsterdam and Utrecht seem quite frequently to lose their personnel to the mainstream media. MOS is planning to develop programmes for minority youth in Dutch.

SEGLO (Utrecht)

SEGLO (*Samenwerkingsverband etnisch groepen-lokale omroep* Cooperation between ethnic groups and local broadcasting) was created because Utrecht minorities felt that the Utrecht local system *Domroep* paid far too little attention to ethnic groups. They now work together and broadcast their programmes on Utrecht's first channel. SEGLO provides programmes in the immigrants' language of origin for Antillians, Arubans, Moroccans, Surinamese and Turks. Information ranks higher than entertainment. Funds come from the ministry and the municipal authorities. SEGLO has its own training centre, and hopes to work together with those institutions in the other three cities.

Adding a few other local initiatives to those of the big four, one can say that a start has definitely been made. Minority broadcasting has gained some influence and trained a group of professionals. However, STOA wants to go much further than this as it fears a lack of permanence in what has been achieved to date and is seeking to develop a permanent minority presence in the media infrastructure of the Netherlands. The Ministry of Welfare, Health and Culture has so far provided the bulk of funds, but threatens every year to withdraw its support. However, a concerted lobby in Parliament has been successful in maintaining the budget. STOA justly fears that government funding will be discontinued as local and regional systems are to become commercial. In that case, audience size will be decisive and will possibly spell the end of information programmes, as well as programmes for small or even tiny ethnic groups. As local authorities have to cut their budgets also, there is little hope of municipalities absorbing the government's role in funding. The latest STOA move is to try and persuade business to adopt migrants' broadcasting organizations as their financial beneficiaries. Although one may conclude that individual local initiatives have generally been successful; acquired knowledge and experience have not yet been shared and accumulated. STOA intends to function as a countrywide support centre in this respect; it wants to co-ordinate courses, set up a communication network and function as a nodal point for documentation and information.

Evaluation

To what extent have the goals of the Dutch minority policy been attained as far as the media (radio and television) are concerned? Insofar as the idea of *multiculturalism* has been its purpose, definite progress was made up to 1989 in that a certain amount of the total air time became available for ethnic groups to report on their major concerns, and for the type of entertainment that they appreciate. After 1989, however, much of this progress was lost. On the other hand, the groups' status within the Dutch broadcasting structure is still only marginal and their programmes so diverse, scattered and restricted in time that it can hardly be called the materialization of the concept of an ethnically pluralist society. Reporters and journalists working within this 'minority playground' are not taken seriously as they find themselves restricted within the confines of the 'ghetto'.

In so far as *social equality* has been the purpose of the Dutch minority policy, the only conclusion is that very little progress has indeed been made. Although it is not easy to pinpoint discrimination, no more than one or two members of ethnic minorities have reached a position of any importance within the national (majority) structure, so that the term 'token gesture' is very appropriate here. As far as the legal status of journalists working on ethnic programmes such as *'Paspoort'* is concerned, one can only speak of 'second-class personnel'. Nor do they seem to have much future within the 'real' broadcasting system, although some aspire to this. The only way out seems to be either to leave 'minority country' behind or start an independent commercial media production company.

In so far as the idea of power and influence is dealt with in Dutch minority policy, considerable gains have indeed been made in the regional and local level broadcasting systems. Ethnic minority representatives are part of the main decision-making bodies, have been enabled to run their own training institutes and courses successfully and have considerably extended their time on the air. At national level ethnic minorities have become part of the media administration and STOA has demonstrated that it is a body with influence.

If one were to ask why, within the span of some ten years, with considerable government support and working in a mood of enthusiasm, the gains have not been more substantial, the answer should be threefold. The first serious drawback has to do with the way in which the minority policy in general has been administered. Too many promising initiatives have been undertaken as short-term projects only. Some have been ill-prepared, funds have not always been secured and the groups for which these projects were envisaged have not always been consulted. I mentioned the VEM project as an interesting endeavour to promote the inclusion of minority women in the media. The project's history is a case in point, in that it is not yet a success. Shortly after its inception the project was in difficulties when the promised funds failed to materialize. Another major problem was the fact that the course members had quite different educational entry-levels. The Studio IM project was abandoned as nobody seemed to have foreseen that ethnic groups working together would not necessarily develop parallel interests and concerns since all belong to minority groups. The history of Studio IM is a painful one as the conflict between those who wanted to construct ethnic identities by raising cultural consciousness (the social workers' approach) and those who wanted to go professional (the journalists' point of view) was never resolved. The Studio is now bankrupt and is regarded as one of the many minority projects that failed. Another major factor is that nobody seems to want to learn from the mistakes of others or to learn from successful experiences. This may be due to the complicated administrative structure of the minority policies, as projects have been sacrificed to bureaucratic incompetence, internal strife and downright power struggles between ministries.

The second drawback explaining the relatively meagre results has to do with the conceptualization of multicultural society itself. As immigrant groups constitute no more than about five per cent of the total population, and are comprised of a large variety of groups, they cannot be expected to become a powerful building block in society as a whole. The Dutch social history of emancipation of religious groups that were big enough to become power factions to reckon with (especially after the introduction of universal suffrage) is simply not a very good example. Further, a central weakness of the whole policy initiative has been the fact that White majority politicians and administrators have been actuating the whole thing rather than responding to genuinely felt and expressed minority needs. One could even argue – this is the central thesis of a recent important PhD dissertation by Jan Rath (1991) – that the idea of lumping people together in one broad 'ethnic minorities' category, and thereby implicitly condemning them as being inadequately equipped for society and unable to overcome disadvantages on their own, is making them jump from the frying-pan into the fire. Whereas the minorities' 'problem' seems to have been racialized ('race relations') in Britain, Rath claims they have been 'minorized' ('ethnic minorities') in Holland.

Finally, an internal contradiction of Dutch minority policy has come clearly into focus in the ethnic media history as told above. The creation of specific ethnic media agencies and projects designed to assist entry into the media establishment has actually put a brake on minorities' opportunities for advancement within the mainstream of Dutch society. Unless there is a change in power relations, minority policies may unintentionally produce ghetto-ization. The third drawback has been the premature interruption of the minority policy between 1979 and 1989. In the mid-1980s there was a collapse of political will in relation to the existing minority policies, fuelled by a nervous belief that they were not producing the desired results. Thus a new minority policy had to be initiated.

'Allochtonous people', integration and the new minority policy

These disappointing results are not very different from what happened to other sections of the Dutch minority policy. Goodwill, lots of money, great effort and enthusiasm do not suffice to bring about a successful result. Unemployment among minorities is alarmingly high – for some groups such as Moroccans and Turks as much as 50 per cent – they are disproportionately dependent on welfare, and very few individual members of minority groups have risen to really important positions in society. The highest-ranking civil servant from a minority group is director of the minorities policy unit at the Ministry of Internal Affairs. Speaking of ghetto-ization, it looks as if minority policies have created their own second-class labour market. The same holds true for other areas of government policy. This has led many Dutch politicians, including Prime Minister Lubbers, to proclaim that the minority policy has failed. There shall be a new approach and the WRR, the influential Government think-tank that designed the minority policy ten years ago, is once again proposing a new policy concept in its 1989 report:

> *Allochtonenbeleid* (social policy for ethnic minority groups). The former minorities are now called the 'allochtons', or 'other' ethnic groups, to show that the government is starting with a clean sheet.

Early in 1991, the Netherlands Government adopted most of the WRR recommendations. The report starts off by recognizing that ethnic minorities were marginalized during the ten years of minority policy. This is attributed to the fact that these very policy programmes have turned ethnic groups into state-dependent categories that have adopted an attitude of waiting rather than one of initiative. The neo-conservative inclinations are obvious: instead of letting them take advantage of what the State offers, it is time to demand something in return from the 'allochtons'. 'Integration' is now the key word rather than 'multi-cultural'. Minorities should learn the Dutch language (even if this may involve a threat to withdraw the welfare cheque), and the struggle against discrimination and racism has been struck off the agenda. The new policy for immigrants is further required to follow the general policy trends of decentralization (municipalities receive more power) and privatization (in order to be able to cut government expenditure).

The mood of the WRR report and of the new government approach is very different from that of 1979. It reflects irritation among large segments of the indigenous population into which immigrants have not yet integrated. 'The White Dutch have done their share, it is now time to expect something in return from the minorities' is the widespread feeling. It is astonishing that the WRR nowhere in its report seriously attempts to fathom the reasons why ten years of minority policy have failed. The reader searches in vain for any discussion in terms of power relations, racism or badly designed programmes. It is a political document rather than a scientific analysis (see the biting comments of ACOM, 1991). No question is asked as to whether some projects and measures have been successful, or could be made so by changing the programme or making a more strenuous effort. The tenor of the times is simply that everything has to be different.

Strength and weakness of the new approach

What can be expected from this new approach that will favour the position of minority groups in the Dutch media? As before, NOS was quick to respond by issuing a new paper in 1990, i.e. *Allochtonen en omroep* (Ethnic minorities and the broadcasting system). This paper reflects the new minority policy clearly as it reasons in terms of integration. Henceforth there shall be special programmes for the biggest groups only, since the smaller ones may now be regarded as integrated or else should find their place within local broadcasting systems. The position of the Dutch language shall be strengthened because minority group members are required to speak Dutch. In general, there shall be less room for culturally specific programming. The Minister for Welfare, Health and Culture too issued a new paper: *Media and Minorities*. Special help for minority groups is now being rejected because the Minister considers that this will lead to inequality between them and native Dutch, thereby running counter to the whole purpose of integration. The Minister agrees with the NOS that minorities should be represented in the broadcasting structure, yet rejects the notion that her Office should engage in positive action on the grounds that this is properly the task of the journalists' trade union rather than of the government. She expects minority organizations such as STOA to take initiatives in this field. She also hopes that NOS will adopt a programme of responsibility *vis-à-vis* minorities, yet she is unwilling to grant them political influence within NOS' legal status. And even more importantly it is proposed that the financing of local minority broadcasting programmes should be discontinued, with municipalities taking their share of the burden from now on.

It would not be too far off the mark to say that ethnic minorities have very little to expect any more from either the government or the national broadcasting system. Finding itself in a defensive position, STOA reacted to all the new developments by organizing a well-attended conference in Utrecht in June 1991 to which Members of Parliament and representatives of labour unions were invited. STOA there proposed a five-year plan to reverse this inimical course of events: it includes the creation of a whole new minority broadcasting system, a comprehensive programme of positive action (*Beleidsplan 1991–1996*) and argues for a more effective training and educational system. All this may turn out to be a last-ditch fight to save minorities from being forced out of the system, yet it could also be a fresh start. Since the government is revealing its intentions without making any promises, minority organizations have a clearer idea of what they are up against. They might dispense with the social workers' approach to the minority problem which has given the whole policy a reputation for unpersuasiveness and become more professional. It also remains to be seen what a possible new militancy and struggle arm in arm with the labour unions will bring in time to come.

References

ACOM (1989): *Een beter beleid? Een reacde op het 'Allochtonenbeleid'* (paper). Leiden.

Bastiaansen, L.M.H. *et al.* (1990): *Minderhedenbeleid, lokale omroepen, een onderzoek naar aktiviteiten van de locale omroepen* (paper). Nijmegen.

Bovenkerk, F. & Bovenkerk-Teerink L.M. (1972): *Sirinamers en Antillianen in de Nederlandse pers.* Amsterdam University, Antropologisch-Sociologisch Centrum.

Lijphart, A. (1968): *The Politics of Accommodation: Pluralism and Democracy in the Netherlands.* Berkeley and Los Angeles, University of California Press.

Rath, J. (1991): *Minorisering de sociale constructie van 'etnische minderheden' in Nederland.* Amsterdam, SUA.

Reinsch, O. P. (1988): *Migrants and the Broadcasting Media in the Netherlands.* Amsterdam University.

Schakenbos, E & Marsman G. (1988): *Migranten en de media*. Nijmegen, Transculturele Uitgeverij Masusa.

STOA (Stichting Omroep Allochtonen) (1991): *Concept Beleidsplan 1991–1996*. Utrecht.

van. Dijk, T.A. (1983): *Minderheden en media, een analyse van de berichtgeving over etnische minderheden in de dagbladpers*. Amsterdam, SUA.

van. Dijk, T.A. (1991): *Racism and the Press*. London, Routledge.

Wiley, N. (1967): The Ethnic Mobility Trap and Stratification Theory. *Social Problems*, Fall, pp. 149–159.

3

Behind the rhetoric: employment practices in ethnic minority media in Australia

Matt Ngui
assisted by Pascal Adolphe, Annette Blonski and
Kalinga Seneviratne

Introduction

This report seeks to examine certain aspects of the development of ethnic minority media in Australia. In particular it aims to focus on the development and employment of technical and professional personnel in the major television, community radio, 'ethnic press' and independent film and video sectors. In examining the employment policies of the majority ethnic media institutions, it is expected that light will be shed on the degree of access that personnel from minority communities have to decision-making and management power within these organizations.

In addition, the report will examine the employment policies and practices of the major minority media institutions in the framework of Australia's multicultural policies and its commitment to equal employment policies in the public and private sectors of the economy. It intends to demonstrate the degree to which ethnic television, radio, print and film media adhere to and implement employment policies within their organizations. Case-studies are used to examine these practices of the major ethnic minority media in Australia.

The report does not set out to examine the content of media representations in Australia.

Background

As Husband observed (1986, 1990), there has been a significant change in the employment of ethnic minority personnel within the dominant media of a number of Western democracies. While much remains to be achieved in the representation of ethnic minority populations by the mass media, it is clear that, in some countries, lobbying by ethnic minority communities, academics and certain non-governmental organizations has increased awareness among media executives. This pressure has not only served to diminish exaggerated stereotypical images of ethnic minorities by the media, but has won space for ethnic minorities to address themselves through the media. Consequently there has been an increase in the number of ethnic minority personnel employed by mass media organizations. However, the results are uneven.

Methodology

The present report is based on face to face interviews with fourteen key personnel working in the Australian Broadcasting Corporation (ABC) and the Special Broadcasting Service (SBS), published papers and articles in media journals, doctoral and masters theses, and two case-studies of the Special Broadcasting Service (SBS-TV and radio), the ethnic press and the independent film and video sector in Australia. These interviews were conducted by researchers in Melbourne and Sydney where the key ethnic and mainstream media institutions are located.

Development of multicultural Australia: immigration and settlement policies: post-war trends in immigration in Australia

Since British colonization, Australia has always been a favourite destination for migrants, and is shaped by the culture and social values of the many homelands from which its migrants came. However, before the Second World War, migrants came mainly from the United Kingdom, so that the dominant culture emerged as British. The Second World War confronted Australia with the dilemma of having a large land mass with a small population, insufficient to sustain itself economically and militarily.

After that War, the number of immigrants increased and the composition of Australia's immigration programme changed dramatically from placing emphasis on selection of persons of British stock to that of persons who were predominantly European. People from European countries besides the United Kingdom, such as Dutch, Germans, Greeks, Hungarians, Italians, Poles and Yugoslavs, came to Australia. They were encouraged to immigrate to Australia in order to help solve the country's diminishing population and provide labour for developing industries. In the mid-1970s the notorious White Australia policy was officially abolished and, since then, Australia has encouraged the entry of migrants from Asian countries.

Australia's population today consists of people from over 100 different countries speaking more than 120 languages. In 1991 Australia's population was estimated to be over 17 million, of which 21 per cent were born overseas. This percentage does not include the children of parents who were born outside Australia: these are estimated to make up another 10 per cent of the population. At current levels of immigration (an average of 120,000 per annum), it is estimated that Australia's population may reach 26 million by the year 2031.

The increase in population reflects the planned approach to population growth through natural increase, augmented by immigration. In the 1990s, in a climate of economic depression, financial constraints and rise in cost of living, added to pressure on the highly urbanized cities of Melbourne and Sydney, the current debate concerns the level of immigration sustainable in Australia. However, without immigration, the Australian Bureau of Statistics has calculated that by the year 2030 Australia will have experienced a negative population growth.

One of the distinguishing features of Australia's current population is the over-representation of overseas-born, and thus by implication immigrants, in all the major cities, particularly Sydney and Melbourne. For instance, over 54 per cent of the total population live in the five major cities, and this figure includes 71 per cent of the immigrants. Another significant feature of immigration in the 1980s was the increasing number of South-East Asians coming to settle. Jayasuriya & Sang (1990) have cautioned readers regarding the different definitions of 'Asian' used by the Australian Bureau of Statistics and the Department of Immigration, Local Government and Ethnic Affairs. Essentially, the former included Egypt, Lebanon and the Middle East, whereas the latter excluded them.

This trend in settler arrivals in Australia in the 1980s has generated intense public feeling with strong racist undertones against 'Asians', mainly Cambodians, Malaysians, Singaporeans and Vietnamese. It has also stimulated the growth of racist organizations in Melbourne, Perth and Sydney. However, in spite of the increasing number of settlers coming from South-East and North-East Asia, the majority of immigrants to Australia continue to come from Europe, particularly the United Kingdom. However, given the changing composition of its population, Australian institutions and structures are reluctantly coming to terms with the diversity of people and new values.

This changing population has confronted Australians with a new social and cultural reality. In 1975 the Labour Government responded to pressure from ethnic groups in view of their impact on electoral politics, their awareness of their exploitation by the manufacturing industry and the growth of ethnic organizations by introducing a new public policy of multiculturalism. To fully understand the development and implications of this policy and ideology, it is necessary to trace the evolution of Australia's settlement policies from the advent of mass immigration following the Second World War.

Australian settlement policies: assimilation and integration

The impact of migrants on Australian society since 1945 and the response by various elected governments have varied depending upon the prevailing state of the Australian economy, and the social, political and economic status of emigrant countries and regions. Australian social policy in the 1950s and 1960s was characterized by benevolent paternalism towards immigrants on the part of society and government. Migrants were expected to integrate into all aspects of Australian life so as to allay the xenophobic fears of the dominant group. The assimilation policy accepted the dominance of White Australia and the necessity for homogeneity to ensure that racial harmony was maintained. Policies of integration required that all immigrants should ignore their identity and cultural origin and become part of the wider Australian society. In the 1970s a new philosophy relating to migrant/host relationships couched in the language of 'cultural pluralism' was identified as an ideology leading to multiculturalism. The new ideology represented a challenge to the cultural dominance of the English and the explicit recognition by the government of the disadvantaged and powerless status of non-British migrants.

Multi-culturalism

In the mid-1970s and early 1980s Australia embraced cultural pluralism. This policy thrust was expounded in a report entitled 'Review of Post-Arrival Programmes and Services to Migrants' (1978). It essentially celebrated ethnic differences in a cultural sense while simultaneously shifting migrant services from the general rhetoric of social welfare to often marginal 'ethnic services'. As a recent study commented:

> The shift in the language for reading cultural difference and formulating settlement and welfare policy was from a unified 'family of nations' to multiculturalism; from disadvantage to difference; from concern with general socio-economic issues in which migrants are implicated to the paradigm of cultural difference in which cultural dissonance is the main problem; from a theory of class as the primary division to a theory of multiple social divisions, none of which have priority (Cope, Castles & Kalantzis, 1991, p. 14).

Between 1972 and 1975, the Federal Labour Government initiated the following changes to settlement policies: pursuit of equality of opportunity for migrants and ethnic groups; emergence of the Ethnic Rights movement; development of organizational structures to perform a variety of roles in ethnic and migrant communities; appointment of migrant members to the Immigration Advisory Council for the first time; development of Task Forces to investigate, consult and report directly to the Minister on a range of issues affecting the well-being of migrants, and the inauguration of ethnic radio in Melbourne and Sydney as a participatory mechanism. This ideology was expressed in policies which emphasized the co-existence of many cultures within a society as the single most significant factor in maintaining harmony.

In the 1980s one of the key features of multicultural policies was the increasing involvement of state governments in response to the social, economic and political impact of immigration. In each state, a Multicultural and Ethnic Affairs portfolio was created and Ethnic Affairs Commissions established to advise the Ministers for Multicultural and Ethnic Affairs. Commissions were enshrined in legislation and involved taking action to safeguard the rights of migrants to fair and equal treatment, particularly in workplaces and access to services.

There is a certain legislative overlap between State Ethnic Affairs Acts and the Equal Opportunity Acts in regards to the rights of migrants. Procedures and penalties for breaches of the Equal Opportunity Acts stand in sharp contrast to the advisory nature of the Ethnic Affairs Acts.

In the late 1980s the Federal Government established the Office of Multicultural Affairs, one of whose major tasks was to identify a multicultural agenda for all Australians that would embody three major dimensions, namely: (1) Cultural identity: the right of all Australians, within carefully defined limits, to express and share their individual cultural heritage, including their language and religion; (2) Social justice: the right of all Australians to equality of treatment and opportunity, and the removal of barriers of race, ethnicity, culture, religion, language, gender or place of birth; (3) Economic efficiency: the need to maintain, develop and utilize effectively the skills and talents of all Australians, regardless of their backgrounds.

This Agenda sets out the multicultural policy thrusts of the Australian Government in terms of access to services, employment opportunities, education, housing and equity in the distribution of public funds for community development. One of the Government's commitments to ethnic minority media was the promise to establish the Special Broadcasting Service (SBS) as an independent corporation. It provides for a charter to define the multicultural and multilingual character of SBS and the extension of its services to Darwin and eight other non-metropolitan centres. This legislation was placed before the Australian Parliament in the spring session of 1991.

Media in Australia

As a nation of 17 million people including 5 million migrants, Australian minority media present unique opportunities and problems. Australia has an enormous land mass of approximately 8 million square kilometres while the distribution of its population is concentrated in and around the six major cities. It experiences a 'tyranny of distance'. Added to this is the 'regionalism' of Australia as a federation of six states, each with a strong sense of local identity. Australian broadcasting and press are thus predominantly regionalized. This has resulted in two major problems: (a) broadcasting is becoming extremely expensive; because of great distances and regional allegiances, Australia has to multiply the transmission of production facilities and ensure services to remote and sparsely populated regions; (b) the broadcasting networks and press are centralized in the major capitals, particularly Sydney and Melbourne, to the detriment of the numerically smaller capitals, rural and remote areas; this control creates inequality in broadcast services provided and in communication distribution.

Australia has 47 commercial television, 3 remote television, and 2 public television channels (Stubbs, 1991, p. 399). Australian Radio holds 219 licenses. Of these 123 are licensed on the AM band and 96 on the FM band. Both television and radio licenses are renewed by the Australian Broadcasting Tribunal (ABT) for periods of from 12 months to 3 years.

The Australian Broadcasting Corporation was founded as the Australian national broadcaster on 1 July 1932 and became a Corporation 53 years later. It is funded by the Federal Government to the amount of $77 million per annum.

ABC television provides a national network service to all capital cities including Australia's remote areas via the satellite service. At the same time metropolitan television stations are now owned by major Australian banks (seven), receivers (ten) and Kerry Packer (nine). The issue of cross-media ownership in the main-stream media is the current obsession in Australia. This scramble to own media institutions was created in part by the demise of many who were victims of the 1989 stock market collapse. Hence ownership regulations are a subject of keen interest to those who anticipate owning a television station. Current ownership regulations in Australia stipulate that a person may not have a prescribed interest (i.e. any direct or traceable interest above 5 per cent in a licensee company) in: (a) commercial television licenses that have a combined audience reach of more than 60 per cent of the nation, or (b) two or more commercial television licenses in the same state or metropolitan area (Stubbs, 1991, p. 395).

Profits in television are generated by selling advertising time during high-rating time-slot periods. The development and extension of the communications industry in Australia has much to do with technological innovation and political economy, so that the main focus in the Australian media industry today is on television.

The survival of the oligopolistic television market is guaranteed by the state. The government grants licenses to all television and radio operators and has until now kept each market quite restricted. All regulatory control rests in the hands of the Department of Transport and Communications. The ABT is the statutory body of that department set up to administer and monitor movement within the industry. However, it has no legislative control. Many inquiries, reports and recommendations have been made over the years in attempts by the government to maintain control over its broadcasting industry. Initially the intention of the legislation governing television operation was to regulate the industry, in contrast to the free market environment operating in the United States. However, the introduction of new telecommunications systems has propelled the Australian broadcasting industry in that very direction. The current contention surrounding the operation of AUSSAT, and the introduction of Pay Television, if approved, may change the direction of the Australian broadcasting system.

Australia's print media constitute a vast and diverse industry of newspaper publications and magazines. The advent of desktop publishing has led to a further expansion of independent publications. There are 23 metropolitan newspapers and 358 regional newspapers in circulation in Australia today. However, it is not possible to gauge circulation numbers, as they are not all available. Currently no restrictions are placed on ownership of the print media, but cross media ownership in the mainstream media is a dominant issue in Australia today.

Australia's private media sector has one of the world's most highly concentrated patterns of ownership. Currently a few large corporations dominate the industry: News Limited, John Fairfax Limited and Australian Consolidated Press. This gives the private media owners considerable economic and political control. Their main concern, in advocacy of the 'free market' system, is currently to exercise their interests in a parliamentary push towards self-regulation of the broadcasting system.

Minority media in Australia

Minority print media

The Ethnic Press is a mediator in a prolonged and varied encounter between languages, cultures, expectations and fears. At the same time it is a link to the institutions of the ethnic community itself, its clubs, societies and co-operatives; the things which maintain cohesion. It advertises jobs, housing and shopping facilities. It may even encourage literature (Geiselhart, 1989, p. 23).

The concept of an ethnic press in Australia is not a recent phenomenon. As early as 1848, the *German Post* was established as the nation's first foreign language newspaper. It had a very short life, but many others have appeared since, and the oldest survivor, *Le Courier Australien*, has been 'catering to Francophiles Down Under since 1892' (Geiselhart, 1989, p. 23). At present, many ethnic newspapers are experiencing difficulties maintaining readership, a problem largely attributed to increasing reliance on the electronic sector of the ethnic media to satisfy the news and information needs of the ethnic communities, as well as to loss of literacy in the community language among the second and subsequent generations of migrants.

The minority print media in Australia is highly segmented by language and region. Currently there are 137 ethnic newspapers in circulation (Victorian Ethnic Affairs Commission, 1990, pp. 13–33). They are divided into three categories: (i) the fully commercial operation consisting of newspapers published as a business venture and driven by the profit motive; (ii) the semi-commercial operation consisting of non-profit making newspapers published and made to financially support all those who work for them, and (iii) the private venture consisting of dedicated individuals or groups with a message to pass on. This is augmented by voluntary effort (Bosi, 1980, p. 34).

The function of the minority press has always been distinct from the other parts of the media. It has primarily been used as an avenue of communication for specific ethnic and other minority groups. The minority press has also functioned for a considerable period of time as the sole linguistic link to their homeland for thousands of non-English-speaking Australians. It continues to provide this service to its readership by acting as a conduit of news from the 'old' country and from other parts of the world. They report on community activities and services and simultaneously assist in maintaining linguistic, religious and cultural traditions. While many minority newspapers have celebrated a long life-span, there is considerable entry and decline in the industry. Each wave of immigrants produces a string of new publications. However, the matter of survival depends upon their ability to reach the second generation.

Bell *et al.* (1989) researched 100 minority newspapers, their editors and owners, and reported the following findings concerning the minority print media sector in Australia:

• It is considered a small business industry with few economies of scale and may be established with the aid of capital.

• Of the 100 newspapers surveyed, 85 per cent were established for at least 5 years; 50 per cent for 10 years or more.

• The newspapers surveyed employ 563 full-time and 256 part-time workers; 11 have more than 20 full-time staff.

• A third of ethnic newspapers are owned by companies and a quarter by individual proprietors; the rest are produced by ethnic community organizations.

• 29 publications have a 'national' readership, 21 are distributed in Sydney and 11 in Melbourne.

• 50 of the newspapers are published less than once a week, 40 each week and 1 twice a week.

• 29 newspapers have print-runs of more than 10,000 copies, while 51 have runs of more than 2,000 copies.

• 36 languages are represented among the 100 newspapers surveyed. Apart from advertising and sales, there is no significant source of revenue for any of the 100 newspapers surveyed.

• Potential readership is estimated at some 2 million.

• Journalists (who are few in this industry) perceive their role as translators, not originators of news items; editors feel constrained by the need to retain advertising revenue.

• Ethnic language publications require more specialized, professionally trained journalists writing on economics, health, women's welfare, business and political issues.

Minority radio

The Australian Broadcasting Corporation broadcasts by radio to all Australians via an international service, Radio Australia. Programmes go out in English to Asia, Europe, North America and the Pacific. Its foreign service broadcasts in eight languages to Africa, Asia, the Gulf States, the Indian Ocean and the Pacific. ABC Radio provides three radio services in all major cities. Rural areas receive one radio service which may be extended to two or three in 1993 when the Regional Radio network is completed. It also provides a national youth network and three shortwave stations beamed at the remote Aboriginal communities in the Northern Territory.

In the years from 1950 to 1974, there was general agreement that immigrants should be encouraged to learn English as quickly as possible rather than form non-English-speaking communities. During those years the foreign-language broadcasting that could be transmitted by commercial radio broadcasters was restricted by the Australian Broadcasting Control Board (ABCB). Radio stations were prohibited from broadcasting more than 2.5 per cent of their programme hours in languages other than English (White, Rosh & White, 1983, p. 140). Because of these restrictions on foreign language broadcasts, and the even more stringent regulations on advertising in foreign languages, most commercial broadcasters were unwilling to take the risk of even devoting the 2.5 per cent of their programme hours to foreign-language broadcasting. The prevailing assessment was that non-English programmes were both undesirable and uneconomic (White, Rosh and White, *op. cit.*). By 1972 the amount of broadcast time devoted to non-English broadcasting had fallen to 36 hours per week for all of Australia.

The Special Broadcasting Service (SBS) was a pioneer in ethnic radio broadcasting in Australia. It broadcasts to the Sydney metropolitan area through 2EA in 59 languages for 126 hours, although this was recently reduced. A similar service is provided in Melbourne. Other cities such as Adelaide, Brisbane and Perth receive radio through relay stations. One of the key issues confronting the SBS model of language-based broadcasting is the rescheduling of programmes necessitated by the rise in demand for air time in excess of what is available. This problem is inherent in the language-based model of public broadcasting as evidenced by the constant need to reschedule programmes to accommodate the demands for air time from groups that are currently excluded from broadcasting.

The Public Broadcasting sector in Australia was established in 1972 when (VL) SUV in Adelaide commenced broadcasting with an experimental licence. In 1974, 2 MBS in Sydney and 3 MBS in Melbourne joined the group. Currently there are 100 licensed public radio stations in the cities, towns and regions of Australia. Public radio stations are locally owned and operated by community-based organizations. They are non-profit and non-commercial and independent of government. The majority of public broadcasters are members of the Public Broadcasting Association of Australia (PBAA). Membership includes a wide range of community and special interest sectors such as Aboriginal, cultural, ethnic, religious and sporting groups.

The advent of ethnic radio has to a large extent distracted attention from the ethnic press. Although minority/ethnic radio broadcasting began on commercial stations in the 1950s, it now operates predominantly through the public broadcasting sector. There are three models of public ethnic radio broadcasting in Australia. They are: (i) the government public sector; the SBS stations 2EA in Sydney and 3EA in Melbourne; (ii) independent public ethnic stations such as: Ethnic 3ZZZ in Melbourne; 4EB in Brisbane; SEBI in Adelaide and 6EBA in Perth; (iii) independent ethnic broadcasting via other public radio stations; 42 public radio stations (other than those mentioned above) broadcast ethnic radio programmes.

It should also be noted that in some rural areas where there are large ethnic populations, air time is allotted for them on commercial stations. Public ethnic radio has been broadcasting in Australia for over fifteen years with the aid of government funds, being the main source of revenue for broadcasters. SUV in Adelaide was the first radio station to put out an ethnic programme.

Although ethnic radio has seen rapid growth over the years, its development and extension cannot be credited to a well-defined and cohesive government policy on ethnic broadcasting: quite the contrary, in fact. Since the government offered to sponsor a three-month ethnic radio experiment on 2EA and 3EA (later to become known as the SBS stations) in 1975, in its interests to sell the Medibank health scheme before elections, the development and extension of ethnic radio has been in a state of uncertainty.

The main advantage of ethnic radio is its efficiency in conveying news about the 'homeland' and the resident community in Australia. However, this is only applicable to ethnic groups that broadcast daily. Groups broadcasting on a weekly or bi-weekly basis are late with news items. The advantage of the ethnic group's press is that it has a greater degree of independence than ethnic radio. The ethnic press has ensured its own survival through advertising; the sole alternative source of income it receives comes from government funds at election time. On the other hand public ethnic radio, in the case of 2EA and 3EA, is fully funded by the government. In the case of independent ethnic stations and other ethnic broadcasters, subsidies are received from the Public Broadcasting Foundation (PBF). In both cases, the government has some influence in controlling what can or cannot be broadcast through its funding guidelines. The processes and policies that have determined the introduction and evolution of ethnic radio may not always have had the best interests of Australian ethnic minority groups at heart.

The major contentions relating to problems of extension have focused on the balance of funding. Like the rest of the Australian media, broadcasting is centralized in Melbourne and Sydney. Due to the high costs of transmission and production it has been difficult to maintain 'access and equity' within the ethnic broadcasting sphere. This means that Melbourne and Sydney, and their regional areas, are provided with a vast and extensive service at government expense. True, these two capitals boast the highest number of ethnic minority groups, but the call for a more balanced allocation of services and funding needs to be addressed.

Public ethnic broadcasters have been granted licenses through the Australian Broadcasting Tribunal and receive a comparatively small annual government subsidy, administered through the PBF. Most of their financial backing comes from donations, sponsorship and the community groups themselves. None the less, public ethnic radio broadcasting has become a success story in Australia. It is cheap to manage because most of its participants are unpaid committed volunteers who approach their objectives with a great deal of commitment. Because all participants, including broadcasters and administrators, are members of a particular ethnic minority group, a shared interest and responsibility exists among those involved. Conversely, much of the money allocated to the SBS stations supports its top-heavy bureaucracy. This fact has led to tension between administrators and programmers, with the latter arguing a conflict of interest. Needless to say, this gap in communication is due to the lack of participation of ethnic minority groups in the decision-making process.

Minority television

The SBS was created on 1 January 1978 by the Federal Government to provide multicultural television services using the sole Very High Frequency (VHF) television network. The station emphasized multicultural and multilingual programming and subtitling with a budget of A$40 million. It is the sole television station dedicated to the cultural and entertainment needs of Australia's ethnic populations. However, television ratings have shown that this aim has not been achieved. On a national average, SBS constitutes approximately 1.5 per cent of viewers. Of these 28 per cent are from non-English-speaking backgrounds, whilst 67 per cent are Australian-born, or come from an English-speaking country (Evans, 1987, p. 19). These figures suggest that SBS does not reach the audience it was intended to serve. White, Rosh & White (1983) support this finding and point to SBS as tending to serve the needs of the majority of the Australian audience.

SBS Television has had to contend with other problems. Since, like the Australian Broadcasting Corporation (ABC), SBS is a public service television broadcaster which attracts a percentage of the TV market, it is regarded as interfering with the high TV revenue returns of the commercial broadcasters. Thus its operations have attracted attention from those who hold economic control of the commercial broadcasting media. ABC and SBS have, therefore, come under close government and public scrutiny. Down the years contentious debates have periodically arisen questioning the funding provisions and statutory rights of both public television stations, even though as yet these two statutory authorities have never competed in the 'mass audience appeal' stakes. Rather has their position been to 'complement' programme formats offered on the commercial channels. Nonetheless, in such circumstances the institution of ABC, as compared with SBS, has two advantages in that it: (i) has a long history of broadcasting based on a British model (the BBC) and has serviced and established the monocultural tradition of Australian broadcasting, and (ii) is much more highly regarded by the majority of Australians who are English-speaking.

These advantageous features of ABC have made it difficult for SBS to establish its credibility. SBS has had to contend with criticism from the public that it is extravagant and wasteful of public funds, while ethnic communities that receive little or no air time claim alleged incompetence and insensitivity to the needs and interests of ethnic groups. In 1986/87 SBS Television fought off threats of amalgamation with ABC, mainly thanks to the ensuing public outcry. When public funding of SBS was cut by the Federal Government, it introduced corporate sponsorship in a bid to increase its revenue.

It is certain now that SBS Television will need to search for additional sources of financial support. SBS receives revenue from sales of merchandise such as documentaries, sub-titled films and books. The process of 'mainstreaming' therefore has begun, and SBS will need to reassess its position both in the television and the radio broadcasting spheres. Recently the Federal Minister for Communication announced the establishment of another 6 VHF television channels for community education. This is to encourage the development of an Open University and provide additional educational and community television for metropolitan Australia.

So far, this report has focused on the broader issues relating to the mainstream electronic media and ethnic minority sector of the industry. It outlines the history and structure of the media in Australia and describes the multi-ethnic nature of the policies that were developed to manage the cross-currents of tensions inherent in such a diverse society. The following section presents two case-studies: (i) the equal opportunity policies of ABC, a mainstream organization, and of SBS, the sole multicultural television station in the country, and, in contrast, (ii) the approach of the independent film and video sector to assessing its accessibility to ethnic minority clients.

Case-study one: employment, training and career

Prospects in SBS and ABC television

Introduction

ABC, as its manual entitled 'Equal employment opportunity programme 1990–1993' stated, is mandated to broadcast innovative and comprehensive programmes that 'contribute to a sense of national identity and inform and entertain, and reflect the cultural diversity of the Australian community'.

In January 1990 all divisions of ABC committed the Corporation's staff to achieving five fundamental goals, entailing more efficient, innovative and effective broadcasting service for all Australians. As a Federal or Commonwealth employer, ABC is legislatively bound by the provisions of the Racial Discrimination Act (1975), the Sex Discrimination Act (1984) and the Human Rights and Equal Opportunity Act (1986). ABC is further required under Section 22B of the Public Service Act to submit an annual Equal Employment Opportunity (EEO) programme report to the Minister for Transport and Communication.

The ABC Equal employment opportunity manual lists a number of its achievements to date in employing Aboriginals, the disabled, migrants and women. In the case of migrants, for instance, ABC lists the employment of multicultural affairs reporters in radio and television news, but does not state the number employed; it also reports the creation of a Multicultural Programme Unit in television. In addition it mentions the establishment of Greek-language programming by SMV in South Australia as another achievement for the national broadcaster.

Employment and training policies and practices in ABC and SBS

The Australian Broadcasting Corporation (ABC)

In respect of employment and training opportunities for people from non-English-speaking backgrounds, ABC and SBS have only recently implemented affirmative action strategies to increase the number of non-English-speaking background staff members to a level that is at least proportional to their percentage representation in the overall Australian community. ABC's Equal Employment Opportunity Programme 1990–1993 has been formulated along similar lines and in response to the same obligations under the Public Service Act as SBS. However, ABC has yet to achieve the EEO policy objectives, given its reluctance to embrace multiculturalism.

A Human Resource Manager at ABC argued that in the current affairs department at ABC Radio, 25 per cent of cadet positions will be targeted at people of non-English-speaking background (NESB). ABC and the Office of Multicultural Affairs (OMA) provide much of the funding for the NESB recruitment programme. ABC has been disappointed with the quality of response to its advertisements for NESB recruits in the past. It has been looking for experienced broadcasters to go on the air for three hours at a stretch, while doing the research and all the preparatory work and at the same time draw the audience.

At the time of writing, ABC's Head Office in Sydney was unable to provide data on the number of its NESB-background employees although a survey was being conducted by the Equal Employment Opportunity Section to obtain this information. On a more positive note, an ABC representative stated that there were many persons with an NESB background in the communication courses and that ABC management was considering a merit selection process to enable it to recruit such personnel having suitable experience in the public radio area.

The Special Broadcasting Service (SBS)

Whilst many SBS presenters have non-British or Aboriginal backgrounds, the ratios for reporters and producers are reverse. Such tokenism only serves to create an 'exotic' appeal for the essentially English-speaking audience. It is not intended to promote access and equality of collection and production of content matter, as this is controlled by Anglo-Australians. Yet section 3.103 of the Report of the Committee of Review of SBS states that 'the multicultural media can make a major contribution to community relations by presenting programmes which reflect the reality of Australia as a heterogeneous and culturally diverse, yet cohesive society. They can help people who have been isolated by their language and their culture to feel part of that society. This can show others that we are all Australians regardless of our diverse backgrounds'. It is worthwhile quoting at this juncture from the SBS Equal Employment Opportunity Programme 1989–1990:

> The Public Service Act, Section 22b, requires each Department to develop an EEO programme designed to ensure that appropriate action is taken to eliminate unjustified discrimination against women and persons in designated groups in relation to employment matters in the department.

The designated groups' are Aborigines and Torres Strait islanders, people of non-English-speaking backgrounds and their children. According to a 1990 EEO survey of SBS's total staff of 800, fully 527 (i.e. 66 per cent) answered a questionnaire on ethnic background. The survey revealed that 45 per cent of its staff were from NESB, and that the radio division of SBS employs the highest proportion of these. This is explained by the fact that the radio network is language-based, i.e. with non-English languages. Of a total of fourteen Senior Executives at SBS, only four were from NESB.

Concern about equal job opportunity at SBS was echoed by many of the journalists working there. One experienced journalist claimed that people of non-English-speaking backgrounds at the TV station were victims of discrimination and even racism which had impeded their career paths to management. 'People like me', he said, 'should have progressed to management level and today SBS should be run by us. But you see, we cannot be trusted, because we are not equal. This society is a racist society. It discriminates against the people that it claims are equal. We are not equal'.

The mainstream agenda, combined with the severe impact of the economic recession, have also affected recruitment at SBS TV, and this in turn has had a detrimental impact on the ethnic communities themselves. The journalist went on to say: 'SBS is becoming a refuge for those losing their jobs in the industry. There are more coming in from the Establishment. People from ethnic backgrounds suffer because they'll never be in charge of the key programmes, the key departments in SBS, and that's news and current affairs'.

Yet another view from SBS TV rejects such accusations of tokenism levelled at SBS recruitment and use of NESB personnel. In the opinion of one SBS TV worker: 'You have to start somewhere and, to be honest with you, tokenism is better than nothing, and it will hopefully lead on to something better'. This person believes that NESB people are already well represented on the overall SBS staff. Yet he admits: 'The jobs that migrants are most likely to fill are part-time, which tends to skew the migrants to the bottom of the salary scale.' As a result, NESBs are not well represented in management and executive ranks because he suspects: 'There is a question of consideration of the relative experience and skill involved. There are five key positions which effect television, and of those only one is filled by an NESB. Two have extensive ABC experience and I think we still have a fair degree of cultural cringe about the ABC, that they train their people well, and if you can't get anybody from the BBC ...'

In Australia, ABC and SBS have a long road ahead to achieve their respective Equal Employment Opportunity targets. The situation in the non-public and mainstream media leaves a lot of room for improvement. As David Ingram, journalism trainer at SBS Radio, asserted at a national media conference in 1989: 'The proverbial visitor from outer space would have difficulty identifying Australia's culture and linguistic or racial diversity if he, she or it relied solely on images from the mainstream media' (Trevitt & Rish, 1989, p. 15).

Commercial media organizations have been reluctant to adopt a multicultural approach to training, production and programming. They continue to construct anachronistic media images that are totally out of touch with the realities of Australian society in 1991.

The overwhelming view of delegates at the 1989 media conference was that, until such time as ethnic and Aboriginal people were part of the executive board in large media organizations like ABC, Fairfax and Murdoch presses, and associated media areas like casting agencies and film and TV production companies, the diverse racial and cultural mix of the country would not be reflected (Trevitt & Rish, 1989, p. 15). And, as Kalinga Seneviratne, a freelance journalist, stated at a 1990 media conference, it was futile discussing commercial TV in this respect because the process of change had to start from SBS and ABC; as long as they indulged in tokenism, the commercial channels would never change.

Case-study two: the independent film and video sector

The sector

Throughout the 1970s and until the mid-1980s, the term 'independent film and video' had a particular connotation. It meant a practice, formally, aesthetically and/or in terms of theme and content, that was an alternative to mainstream cinema. That it relied almost entirely upon government subsidy at both production and distribution levels was a contradiction, a paradox often remarked upon but regarded none the less as essential for its survival. Generally speaking, however, it was the film industry that addressed the more sensitive political questions about Australian culture such as racism, the history of the Aborigines and the place of women in our culture. It tended to reflect upon the greater diversity of cultures within Australia, unlike the mainstream industry which tended to present Australian identity as essentially homogeneous and, with a degree of nostalgia, as White, masculine and Anglo-Celtic. The use of the term 'independent' now encompasses all the companies, groups and individuals who produced programmes outside, rather than within, the major television broadcasters of Film Australia. For television they produce drama (series, serials, telemovies and mini-series), documentaries and light entertainment.

For theatrical (cinema release) and non-theatrical distribution and exhibition, they produce feature films, short dramas, documentaries, experimental/avant-garde work (often with the mass media) and corporate and training videos. There are, however, differences between these groups and individuals, and they may conveniently be divided in two.

Firstly, there are those known as 'the majors' which produce drama, documentary and light entertainment for the commercial television networks and increasingly for ABC and SBS. Their programmes are either co-produced with the network (particularly in the case of the former), or else the producers will raise money through presales, direct investment or distribution guarantees. Some of the majors also develop and produce feature films. For this they seek the support of government funding bodies either to cover their development costs (script development, pre-production and fund-raising), production investment or marketing support. In a shrinking market with reduced government funding, these companies are increasingly powerful and competitive because they can more readily tap into overseas sources of investment and establish longer-term production contracts with broadcasters, producing large blocs of programming. The majors have a small core staffing establishment of producers, usually partners in the company and administrative assistants. All the creative work apart from script development, production and post-production is contracted out to freelancers. Often they draw on the same pool of people, thus building up a team, but they hire their crew on a project-by-project basis. There is also a degree of vertical integration with some companies acting as producers, distributors of their own and other programmes, and as exhibitors.

By far the majority of the sector (in numerical terms) is made up of small-scale producers and individuals who are largely responsible for the feature films and the majority of documentaries produced in this country as well as corporate and training videos. Increasingly, they themselves are being contracted by the majors to work for them, but most try to retain their independence. Some individual film makers, when producing a feature film, short drama or documentary set up a production entity that only lasts for the life of the project. Other production companies are rather more long-term in nature and succeed in maintaining a continuity of funding at the development stage for drama and documentary. In some instances, their work is more adventurous in terms of the subjects they tackle or more innovative than the programmes produced by the majors. The difficulty they face is that they cannot produce large blocks of programming and are forced to sell their programmes on a one-off basis in what is at present a very difficult market with funding reduced in the public sector and the commercial networks straining under substantial debt burdens. If their work is indeed more adventurous, their difficulties are further exacerbated because they are regarded as non-commercial, suitable only for limited audiences and thus ignored by the commercial networks and film distributors. There is only a very limited theatrical market for documentaries at the moment. Hence the reliance on television. However, the picture is looking up for low-budget features, with the conspicuous success of films such as Aleksi Vellis's *Nirvana Street Murders* exhibited in specialist art-house cinemas and carefully targeted so that they can find their audience.

In the past five years, little or no drama has been produced in-house by any broadcasters. Drama is therefore produced by the independents under contract or license. SBS, for instance, has recently invested in the 'Six-Pack' series produced by Bob Weis through his own production company, and will be producing 'Under the Skin', an independently produced series put together by Franco de Chiera with investment from SBS, Film Australia and private sources.

Finally, there are a number of government institutions that are sources of investment and subsidy to this sector. The Australian Film Commission (AFC) supports several low-budget features (funding them fully or partly), short drama, documentary and script development. It also funds cultural activities, marketing and research and gives policy advice to the Federal Government on film and broadcasting from a budget of approximately A$10m per annum. Because of their policy of fully or substantially funding low-budget features, the amount of subsidy lift for short drama, documentary and script development has declined in the past two years. This could have serious implications for film makers from minority backgrounds because many of them, on graduating from film schools, used to make their first foray into the independent sector by making short films or documentaries with the support of AFC. It is difficult to see how film-makers directing their first short film, like Tracey Moffat (for *Nice Coloured Girls*), Luigi Acquisto (for *Spaventepasseri*) and Aleksi Vellis, will be nurtured in the future given the continuing levels of contraction.

AFC has no specific policy relating to multiculturalism in its funding policy, industry strategies, employment of staff within the organization, or general policy formation. This is in sharp contrast to the Australia Council, the major arts funding body in Australia. AFC does not collect statistics on the question of minority film makers.

The Film Finance Corporation (FFC) replaced the IOBA Tax Incentive Scheme in 1998 as the primary source of commercial investment for production. Its government annual allocation of A$67m provides for investment in drama, documentaries and children's television and regards itself as a purely commercial investment house. It states that its criteria for selection at all levels is purely market-driven and commercial, hence it rejects any other policy intervention. Additionally all states except Tasmania have film councils providing projects or script investment and support for training. None of them have a policy relating to multiculturalism or ethnicity.

A survey of the staffing of all of these public institutions and their board members shows that only about 5 per cent come from a minority background. As may be inferred from the above, this sector is quite volatile. In times of recession or of reduction in government support for public broadcasting of film production, the sector goes into rapid decline. It is a freelance industry, approximately 80 per cent of those working there being contractors or self-employed.

The minorities in independent film and video

No figures exist indicating the ethnicity of those employed in the independent film and video sector. No demographic data, apart from those relating to job classification, income and on occasion gender, are collected by any of the institutions involved in research. One notable exception is the 'Survey of Women in Film Television and Video Production' (published in 1987 by the Australian Film Commission and the Australian Film, Television and Radio School) which noted that only 8 per cent of women came from non-English-speaking backgrounds. It is estimated that of directors, 13 per cent were either overseas-born, first generation Australian of non-English-speaking background or Aboriginal; of producers, the figure was 14 per cent; cinematographers 10 per cent; writers 7 per cent; and editors 11 per cent of key creative personnel.

The implications of the freelance nature of employment are profound. Negotiating terms and conditions of employment is difficult and it means that, as contractors of self-employed persons, film and video workers rarely have long-service leave, sick leave or superannuation entitlements; and as there is virtually no provision for child care, defining a career structure is extremely difficult. However, the Victorian Arts and Entertainment Industry Training Board has just completed an industry skills audit of the independent film and video sector. It hopes that having defined the functions of development, production and post-production, it can help to define career paths, set industry standards and facilitate recognition of training. Therefore, when it comes to questions of access and equity for minorities, it is difficult to legislate or indeed monitor. Career prospects in a freelance industry cannot be discussed in the same way as for persons employed full-time in an organization such as ABC or on a newspaper. No organization or research group has attempted to study the employment and participation of minorities in the sector. Unlike the other arts (such as the performing arts, the visual arts, literature, etc.) or even ABC or SBS, no policies have been developed or have trickled down as a result of the National Agenda or the work of groups such as the Office of Multicultural Affairs.

Career advancement

Basically, there are three groups that need to be addressed separately because their experiences differ. The first group are Aboriginal film-makers. The second group are adult migrants (from non-English-speaking backgrounds), by far the greatest number of whom came from Eastern Europe (including Hungary, Poland, Romania, the former USSR and Yugoslavia) before the fall of the Berlin Wall. There are also several people from the People's Republic of China and Viet Nam, although they constitute a tiny minority. Finally, the vast majority are those who come from non-English-speaking backgrounds but were either born in Australia or who came here as children or teenagers.

Career advancement for everyone in the sector depends on a number of factors. The first is experience and evidence of this; the second is networking, i.e. developing a range of contacts and groups of co-workers. People from minority backgrounds who try to enter the industry with overseas qualifications find these two factors particularly hard to negotiate.

Non-English-speaking migrant adults have mixed success in Australia. Almost all were trained in film schools in their country of origin and moved from there straight into the state studio systems. Their experience of film-making is therefore antithetical to the freelance, capitalist structures of Australia. They find the role of government in the sector here very confusing when they first arrive as they expect it to perform the same function as it did in Eastern Europe, for example. In Australia the government supports the industry by means of subsidy, broadcasting content regulations and some funding for Film Australia, a production house for documentaries and some drama. Film Australia has evolved over the past three years from a purely government studio into a private company.

Technicians find it easier to make the transition, whereas qualifications from a film school, whether overseas or local, do not lead directly to employment here. Technicians therefore are able to demonstrate their skill through show-reels and by hands-on work. Editors and cinematographers (Yuri Sokol and Vladimir Osherov are examples) have been able to integrate fairly rapidly by initially working in the low-budget sectors and in small production-cum-training institutions such as Open Channel. From there many have moved into more mainstream production. Those with the greatest difficulty are writers and directors who wish to develop their own projects or obtain work on productions. Their qualifications are not recognized. Moreover, AFC and state film bodies will not provide funding for translations of their previous work, but only for scripts written in English. This means that their writing cannot be assessed.

In one case, a writer had his plays examined and some poetry translated with the assistance of the Victorian Ministry for the Arts. However, he found that he could not use this to make an application to AFC for script development. As most writers and directors in recent years have come from the Eastern bloc, they have been unable to bring their films with them so as to prove their worth. Adult migrants from any non-English-speaking background face the barrier of lack of institutional support from film bodies. They find this particularly frustrating because the industry here is structured in ways that are quite different to their own. The way they write scripts, the stories they tell and their cultural referents are alien to Australian film bureaucrats and employers who insist that they conform to Australian expectations. There is no programme of familiarization or education directly supported by, for instance, AFC or Film Victoria.

The film makers may, at their own expense, attend seminars and workshops conducted by groups such as Open Channel, or the Australian Film Television Institute in Perth, and these organizations are sympathetic to the problem. Their staff and project officers often provide moral support and advice and will try to find employment for them on productions. However, the short courses they conduct are quite expensive (A$200 to A$1,000) and require participants to have a reasonably high level of English language skills. There is no programme of fee subsidy specifically for migrant film makers by any of the film funding bodies. They have to compete for support with local film makers and therefore usually miss out. Some migrants have made contact with each other and try to develop projects co-operatively or simply give each other encouragement. However, they often come from quite different backgrounds and there are too few of them to constitute a strong political lobby. Most of such writers and directors drive taxis or do manual work to earn a living. Some continue to write. Recently one woman managed to make contact with a producer and writer as her English had advanced sufficiently. Together they wrote a script which was successful in obtaining funding from AFC. Another director is making a video about his homeland.

This brings us to the third and major entry point into the industry, in other words training. For all the groups described above – migrant film-makers, aboriginal film-makers and those who are Australian and come from a minority background – formal training is becoming more accessible and increasingly essential. In the educational context, arguments about participation, access and equity have led to training institutions taking in a greater proportion of persons from non-English-speaking backgrounds than they did five years ago. At Swinburne Institute of Technology, for instance, they make up about 30 per cent of the students in both the undergraduate and graduate programmes.

On-the-job training has declined rapidly in Australia since the early 1980s and is therefore no longer the common entry point into the industry. This has opened the way for minority groups as selection for on-the-job training programmes was in the hands of the network administrators. Selection at tertiary institutions, TAFE and the film schools has proved much less of an impediment for minority groups. The growth of formal training, combined with the existence of SBS, has enabled persons from minorities to enter an industry that is predominantly Anglo-Celtic and, as indicated above, many of whose institutions have either no policy in relation to multiculturalism or have only recently begun to address the issue.

In the training sector there appears to be a high degree of sensitivity to the issue now. In 1990, for example, the Australian Film, Television and Radio School (AFTRS) organized a seminar on multiculturalism and script writing attended by representatives of government, industry and a large number of film-makers from a variety of backgrounds. The seminar was part of a strategy to encourage writers to recognize the cultural diversity of Australia in the hope that scripts would begin to tackle this issue. AFTRS has also made it a policy to bring writers from non-English-speaking and minority backgrounds into its screen-writing programme. It also argues with some justification that its intake for the full-time programme increasingly reflects the diversity of Australia's culture. Students gain an understanding of the practice of the film culture and industry they will be entering on graduation and of the fact that familiarity is crucial, as adult migrant film-makers can attest. Students also network with each other, their tutors and visiting film-makers, developing connections and contacts that help them on graduation. This kind of informal education is just as vital as the training programme itself.

One rare success story of an adult migrant is that of a young woman graduate of a film school in the People's Republic of China. Her qualifications were not accepted here although they helped to confirm her status as a film-maker. Despite her rudimentary English, she persisted and finally gained entry into Swinburne Institute where she completed the course. Her English rapidly improved, she made contact with people working in the industry and the short student film she made enabled her to obtain work with SBS. As a migrant film-maker, through access to training, she was able to make the transition. It is worth noting that had SBS not existed this film-maker feels that she would have found it difficult to gain employment on graduation because the sector is chiefly Anglo-Celtic and not sympathetic either to the programmes she wants to make, or to her as an Asian.

The full impact of the entry of minority film-makers into the sector will probably not be felt for several years. AFTRS and Swinburne Institute estimate that their graduates do not reach their peak until some time after graduation, particularly as writers and directors. One measure of what is happening in the sector is given by the growing levels of participation. Greater numbers are being trained and employed but it is necessary to impress upon the funding and policy institutions that institutional and cultural impediments are faced by minority film-makers. Follow-up is also essential to determine what happens to graduates once they leave the training institutions and try to find employment or develop their own projects. The evidence suggests that film-makers from a non-English-speaking background, and first or second generation Australians, find it no harder to gain employment than their counterparts, but this is purely anecdotal. As yet, few Aboriginal film-makers work in the sector in the centre of production (Melbourne and Sydney) but are increasingly gaining access to programme-making in the regional centres. Adult migrants find a niche only with great effort and they tend to be the exceptions rather than the rule. As we have no data, there is no way of properly assessing any of this information. Employment is only half the story. From discussions with many writers and directors it is clear that, apart from developing programmes specifically for SBS, they are finding it difficult to gain the support of the funding bodies for their short and feature films. This is particularly the case when they deal with the experience of migrants in Australia, or of minorities, in a way that is challenging or confrontational in its handling of racism or cultural difference. When the work is not strictly realistic or naturalistic in form, the resistance is even greater.

The question then arises as to whether greater levels of participation and more equitable access will result in any major shift in the kinds of programmes that are made in Australia, including those dealing with cultural difference. Until the institutions themselves begin to grapple with these issues, film such as these will only be made against the odds.

Conclusion

This report of the employment policies and career prospects of personnel from the ethnic minority populations who are working in the television, radio, print and film sectors of the media industry in Australia demonstrates that although there are increasing numbers employed, they are not occupying senior or key positions in SBS or the ABC. Both institutions follow the letter of the law in relation to the government's Equal Opportunity policy, but the reality as perceived by those who work within the institutions indicates that tokenism continues to pervade employment practices. The training and career development of these organizations for employees continues to be of low priority and, where it exists, training has been relegated to technical and less important, non-managerial positions.

From the policy perspective, ethnic media in Australia continue to reflect the model of cultural pluralism of the 1960s and 1970s with its emphasis on languages, the key to understanding any culture. This model of public policy is dysfunctional in the 1990s, except in relation to the new communities that recently joined the 5 million immigrants to Australia. The second generation children of immigrants are English- or Australian-speaking, and are concerned with issues of equity, access to power, discrimination, identity, education, employment and interest rates like other Australians.

Another policy implication of this report is the surprising reluctance or inability of ABC, the national broadcaster, and SBS, the sole multicultural television station in Australia, to reflect the ethnic diversity of contemporary society there. The same may be said of all mainstream media. A recent study by the University of Technology in Sydney found that there was substantial evidence to support this conclusion and that, although there were occasional innovations and attempts to grasp difficult topics, these were not sustained once the momentary gain had waned (Goodall *et al.*, 1990).

Such conclusions reflect the need for all media, including ABC and SBS TV, press and radio, to be given positive encouragement to recruit, employ and promote people from ethnic minorities and the Aboriginal communities, bearing in mind the tendency of media organizations to report the world in their own image.

References

Abe, L., Wade, A. & Ryan, C. (1989): *The Ethnic Press in Australia*. Sydney, Academia Press and Footprints Publications.

Anon (1989): Employment policy for ABC. DEET *Aboriginal News*, April.

Anon (1989): Ethnic Radio ready to hit air waves. *Multicultural Marketing News*, No. 9, p. 3.

Anon (1990): Italianvitation: bringing Australia and Italy closer. *Multicultural Marketing News*, No. 12, p. 6.

Anon (1990): SBS (3EA) Ethnic Radio Station. *Chinese Herald*, No. 14, 29 June.

Anon (1990): Sponsorship and advertising on SBS Television. *Ethnic Spotlight*, No. 20, p. 5.

Anon (1988): Training agreement with CAAMA/Imparja. *Aboriginal Employment and Education News*, No. 16, pp. 4–5.

Anon (1990): Ethnic communities against commercialisation of SBS. *Viet-Luan*, 3 August, p. 17.

Anon (1990): Pay TV for Ethnic Communities. *Australian Chinese Daily*, 22 July, p. 3.

Anon (1990): Vietnamese Press: a lively medium for reaching a community. *Multicultural Marketing News*, No. 12, p. 4.

Atkins, E. (1984): *The media and equality for ethnic people*. FECCA, proceedings of the National Congress, pp. 219–230.

Australian Broadcasting Corporation (1988): Radio and Radio Australia. Equal Opportunity Programme, 1988–89. Internal publication.

Australian Broadcasting Corporation (1990): *Equal Employment Opportunity Programme, 1990–93*. Internal publication.

Australian Institute of Multicultural Affairs (1986): *Multicultural Television*, Melbourne.

Australian Committee of Review of the Special Broadcasting Service (1985): *Serving Multicultural Australia: The Role of Broadcasting*. Canberra, Australian Government Printing Service.

Barbara, K. (1989): Tortuous path to get change: New hit at racism. *The Journalist*, October, p. 7.

Beatson, J. (1990): New report urges faster development for public TV stations in Australia. *Australian Financial Review*, 5 June, p. 48.

Bednall, D.H.B. (1988): Television Use by Melbourne's Greek Media. *Information Australia*, 47, pp. 44–49.

Bell, P., Heilpern, S., McKenzie, M. & Pond, J. (1989): *Different Agenda: Economic and Social Aspects of the Ethnics Press in Australia*. New South Wales, Social Impacts.

Bosi, P. (1980): Ethnic Press: A Question of Survival. In: Mayer (ed.). *Media Information Australia*. Sydney, Australian Film and Television School, February.

Bostock, L. (1989): The Aboriginal Perspective on Multiculturalism in Ethnic Community Councils of NSW. *National Media Conference*, pp. 32–35.

Bureau of Immigration Research (1990): *Consolidated Statistics 1989–1990*, No. 18.

Bureau of Immigration Research (1990): *Consolidated Statistics 1989–1990*, No. 16.

Byrnes, J. (1988): *Enterprises in Aboriginal Australia: Fifty Case Studies*. Armidale, University of New England, Rural Development Centre.

Cauchi, M. (1988): The ABC Multicultural Programmes Unit. *Ethnic Voice 1*, No. 7, pp. 12–13.

Christaki, C. & Gardini A. (1987): *Ethnic media report*. South Australian Ethnic Affairs Commission.

Committee of Review of the Special Broadcasting Service (1985): *Report*, AGPS, 4 Vols.

Cope, B., Castles, S. & Kalantzis, M. (1991): *Immigration, Ethnic Conflicts and Social Cohesion*. University of Wollongong, Centre for Multicultural Studies, New South Wales.

Corker, J. (1989): Broadcasting for Remote Aboriginal Communities Scheme (BRACS): Destined to Fail? *Media Information Australia*, No. 51, pp. 43–44.

Davis, G. (1988): *Breaking up the ABC*. Sydney, Allen and Unwin.

Department of Employment and Training (1989): Employment policy for the ABC. *Aboriginal News*, April.

Delacy, A. (1985): Radio and TV in a multicultural society. In: *Federation of Ethnic Communities' Councils of Australia. First National Congress, Sixth National Conference and AGM*. Melbourne, pp. 105–107.

Department of Aboriginal Affairs (1986): Aboriginal Broadcasting and Communications. *Aboriginal Affairs Background Notes*. AGPS.

Department of Communications (1982): *The Extension and Development of Ethnic Radio*. Discussion Paper, AGPS.

Department of Immigration, Local Government and Ethnic Affairs (1991): *At a Glance*. AGPS, February.

Di Mascio, J. (1985): *Ethnic media in New South Wales*. A guide to the ethnic media in New South Wales for use by government liaison, publicity and information officers. 4th ed. Sydney, Premiers Dept.

Ethnic Television Review Panel (1980): *Programming for the Multicultural/Multilingual Television Service*. AGPS, Second Report.

Evans, H. (1987): Prospects for the SBS. In: Mayer (ed.). *Media Information Australia*. Sydney, Australian Film and Television School, November, pp. 17–22.

FECCA (1990): Federation's position on the Special Broadcasting Service, p. 3.

Foster, L. & Stocking D. (1984): *Multiculturalism: The Changing Australian*. Paradigm Colomway Press.

Fox, C. (1990): Assimilation cuts into ethnic press market. *Australian Financial Review*, 5 June.

Geiselhart, K. (1989–90): Lots of Variety in this Spice of Life. *Kurier Zachodni*, Nos. 34, pp. 23–24.

George, S. (1990): SBS Aims for more Australian Content. *Encore*, February.

Goodall, H., Jakubowicz, A., Martin, J. & Seneviratne. K. (1990): *Racism, Cultural Pluralism and the Media*: A report to the Office of Multicultural Affairs. Sydney, University of Technology.

Heidt, E. II. (1987): *Mass Media, Cultural Tradition and National Identity: The case of Singapore and its Television programmes*. Saarbrucken/Fort Lauderdale. Breitenbach Publishers.

Husband, C. (1986): Mass Media, Communication Policy and Ethnic Minorities: An Appraisal of Current Theory and Practice. In: *Mass Media and the Minorities*. Bangkok, UNESCO Regional Office.

Husband, C. (1990): *The Development of Ethnic Minority Media in Western European Countries: a Research Proposal*. Unpublished.

Ingram, D. (1989): A view from a room: a newcomer's view of Multiculturalism in the Media. In: *Ethnic Community Councils of NSW*. National Media Conferences, pp. 23–31.

Jakubowicz, A. (1987): Days of Our Lives: Multiculturalism, Mainstreaming and 'Special' Broadcasting. *Media Information Australia*, No. 45, pp. 18–32.

Jakubowicz, A. (1989): Australian Media – Does 'Access and Equity' Exist? In: *Ethnic Community Councils of NSW*. National Media Conference, pp. 49–50.

Jayasuriya, D.L. (1985): Multiculturalism in Australia. *Ethnos*, May, NSW Ethnic Affairs Commission.

Jayasuriya, D. L. & Sang, D. (1990): Asian Migration. *Current Affairs Bulletin*, May.

Jennett, C. (1988): The Mass Media. In: *The Australian people: an encyclopaedia of the nation, its people and their origins*. Sydney, Angus and Robertson, pp. 252–255.

Johnson, L. (1984): The ABC and multiculturalism. *Island Magazine*, No. 21, pp. 14–16.

Kee, P. & Mackiewicz, G. (1986): *Community Media Habits and Social Relations: Adelaide before the Arrival of Multicultural Television*. Melbourne, Australian Institute of Multicultural Affairs.

Kilborn, R. (1989): They don't speak proper English: A new look at the dubbing and subtitling debate. *Journal of Multilingual and Multicultural Development*, 10, No. 5, pp. 421–434.

Kissane, K. (1988): Ethnic press alive and well. *Time Australia*, 3, No. 11, p. 32.

Koutsoukas, C. (1989): Multiculturalism and the Broadcasting Media. In: *Ethnic Community Councils of NSW*. National Media Conference, pp. 36–39.

Lauer, P. K., Hall, J. & Cryle, D. (1987): *Aboriginal, Alien Ethnic*. Brisbane, Brisbane History Group.

Lewins, F. (1984): Putting politics into ethnic relations. In: J. Jupp (ed.). *Ethnic politics in Australia*. Sydney, George Allen and Unwin.

Molnar, H. (1990): Aboriginal Broadcasting in Australia: Challenges and Promises. *Howard Journal of Communications*, 2(2), pp. 149–169.

Nicholson, S. (1989): The Australian Journalists' Association. In: *Ethnic Community Councils of NSW*. Sydney, National Media Conference, pp. 45–48.

Office of Multicultural Affairs (1990): *Youth, Media and Multiculturalism: A review of literature*. Canberra, Ken Strahan, August.

Patterson, R. (1988): *The Special Broadcasting Service and the Construction of Ethnic Radio and Multicultural Television*. Griffith University, PhD Thesis.

Rando, G. (1985): Multilingual Radio in South Australia. *Media Information Australia*, Feb/Mar., pp. 41–48.

Rando, G. (1985): Multilingual Programmes on Victorian Radio. *Media Information Australia*.

Senate Standing Committee on Education and the Arts (1987): *The proposed amalgamation of the ABC and the SBS*. AGPS Report.

Seneviratne, K. (1990): *Is the Australian Media Accessible to Diverse Viewpoints?* Unpublished paper.

Seneviratne, K. (1989): Diversity and Access in the Media. *Infocus*, 13, No. 23, pp. 7–9.

Sievers, K.R. (1990): Audience Measurements for Special Purpose Television. *Broadcasting Media Information Australia*, 56, pp. 15–21.

Spurgeon, C. (1989): Challenging technological determinatism: Aborigines, Aussat and remote Australia. Bibl. in *Australian communications and the public sphere: Essays in Memory of Bill Bonney*, pp. 27–45.

Stefanik, H. (1989): Ethnic public broadcasting: a place in the multicultural sun? In: *Ethnic Community Councils of NSW*. National Media Conference, pp. 40–44.

Stocker, E. (1984): *A History of Multilingual Broadcasting in Sydney and Melbourne, Australia (1975–1980)*. San Francisco State University, MA Thesis.

Storer, D. (1988): Policy Implications of Australian Sub-study on Information Needs and Requirements of Migrant Workers. In: T. Hujanen (ed.). *Joint Study on The Role of Information in the Realisation of the Human Rights of Migrant Workers* (Conclusions and Recommendations). University of Tampere.

Stubbs, S. (1991): *The Book of Australia: Almanac 1991–92*. Sydney, The Watermark Press.

Sykes, R. B. & Sykes R.B. (1986): Technological change and black Australian culture: threat or challenge. In: *Science, Technology and the Law*. Speeches from the symposium on 'The Law and the Future: The Impact of Scientific and Technological Change'. Melbourne.

Tenezakis, Md. (1984): *The Neglected Press: A Study of Arab and Greek Newspapers and their Sydney Publics*. AGPS.

Toyne, P. (1986): *The development of local television broadcasting units in central Australia*. Projects Report Commonwealth Scientific and Industrial Research Organisation, Division of Wildlife and Rangelands Research No.3, Paper 3. 15, pp. 1–3.

Trevitt, L. & Rish B. (1989): Why is Ramsay Street full of Anglos? National Media Conference. *Infocus*, 13, No. 25, pp. 12–15.

Tzannes, R. (1990): Multicultural community radio. *Ethnic Spotlight*, No. 19, p. 18.

Van der Weel, A. (1990): Subtitling and the SBS Audience. *Media Information Australia*, No. 56, pp. 22–26.

Venner, M. (1988): Broadcasting for Remote Aboriginal Communities Scheme. *Media Information Australia*, No. 47, pp. 37–43.

Victorian Ethnic Affairs Commission (1990): *A Guide to Ethnic Media in Australia*.

White, N. R. & White, P.B. (1983): *Immigrants and the Media*. Case Studies in Newspaper Reporting. Melbourne, Longman Cheshire.

White, N. R. & White, P.B. (1988): The Mass Media and Immigration. In: *The Australian People: an encyclopaedia of the nation, its people and their origins*. Sydney, Angus and Robertson, pp. 910–1013.

Young, C. (1986): Ethnic Media and Ethnic Groups: Ethnic media use and newspaper readership among Turkish, Yugoslav, Greek and Arabic communities in Australia. *Media Information Australia*, No. 40, pp. 49–55.

Young, C. & Taylor, J. (1985): *The Turkish and Yugoslav Press: A survey of content and readership of ethnic newspapers in Melbourne*.

Zelinka, T. (1990): Multicultural Community Radio Association. *Infocus*, 14, No. 4, p. 12.

Zolf, D. (1989): Comparison of Multicultural Broadcasting in Canada and four other countries. Bibl. in *Canadian Ethnic Studies*, 21, No. 2, pp. 13–26.

4

Access to the media and the challenge to cultural racism in France

Pascale Boucaud and Paul Stubbs

In this chapter we have two complementary views of the relationship of ethnic minorities to the mass media in France. Boucaud provides a broad insight into the range of media activity engaged in by ethnic minorities in France and sketches in outline some of the institutional means which support this activity. Her examples develop this analysis in relation to specific ethnic communities. Stubbs, on the other hand, as an outside observer, provides a different, and complementary view, in this case-study of the activities of IM'média.

France has a strong tradition as a demotic-unitarian nation-state in which citizenship in its conception and institutionalization is indivisible. Ethnicity formally plays no part in determining French citizenship, and the state has resisted constructing a bureaucratic infrastructure to facilitate recognition of and provision for ethnic minorities within France. 'La tradition centraliste française interdit la reconnaissance dans l'espace public des «communautés», au sens où elles existent aux États-Unis' (The French centralist tradition proscribes any recognition of 'communities' in society in the sense in which they are found in the United States) (Schnapper, 1990, p. 251).

At the same time the emergence in post-Second-World-War France of a de facto multi-ethnic society has generated tensions within a society already undergoing significant change. Given its self-image France has had difficulty in confronting the growing racism within its borders (Taguieff, 1991); and this ambiguity has contributed to the success enjoyed by Le Pen (Taguieff, 1991; Harris, 1990; Vaughan, 1991). As national cultural identity has become central to a racialized nationalism, the question of ethnic minorities determining their own media representation has become all the more critical.

I. FRENCH MINORITIES AND ACCESS TO MEANS OF COMMUNICATION
Pascale Boucaud

Introduction

The means of communication are one of the most powerful bulwarks of our fundamental liberties. No social group or state can be the exclusive owner of all that human beings yearn for, e.g. the good, the just and the true. And in a democratic and pluralist society, nobody should attempt to impose his views on anyone else. Everyone therefore can freely express – by any means – his or her own basic opinions. Thus the power of the word can take over from the word of the powerful.

The above is in strict compliance with article 10 of the European Convention of Human Rights and Fundamental Liberties:

1. Everyone has the right to freedom of expression. This right shall include freedom to hold opinions and to receive and impart information and ideas without interference by public authority and regardless of frontiers. This article shall not prevent States from requiring the licensing of broadcasting, television or cinema enterprises.

2. The exercise of these freedoms, since it carries with it duties and responsibilities, may be subject to such formalities, conditions, restrictions or penalties as are prescribed by law and are necessary in a democratic society, in the interests of national security, territorial integrity or public safety, for the prevention of disorder or crime, for the protection of health or morals, for the protection of the reputation or rights of others, for preventing the disclosure of information received in confidence, or for maintaining the authority and impartiality of the judiciary.

The ethnic minority press

In France the written press of foreign origin or language is submitted to different regulations from those of the French press. Article 14 of the 21 July 1881 Law, amended by a decree ('décret-loi') of 6 May 1939, stipulates the principle of free circulation of the press, but allows the Ministre de l'Intérieur (Home Office minister) to prohibit by decree the 'circulation, dissemination and sale of papers, periodical or non-periodical writings, written in a foreign language or written in French but of foreign origin, printed abroad or in France'. This prerogative is only exceptionally taken advantage of. The circulation of the foreign press in France is therefore fairly free. Apart from the publications in French sometimes issued by the official services of foreign embassies or representations, two categories of publications can be considered as relevant to our topic.

The first category includes those publications published abroad for immigrants living in France. Hardly any specific publications are issued by neighbouring countries in so far as their own press freely enters France and satisfies most of their nationals' information needs. There is though *L'Algérien en Europe* (The Algerian in Europe) written in French by the Algerian official services and a comparable Portuguese publication. The Jewish communities have permanent access to publications in Hebrew or Yiddish. Some old publications in Russian are still alive, but the most enduring remains the old Polish press. It includes, besides a daily paper published in Lens (France), *Narodowiec*, founded in 1909 and still with a circulation of several thousand copies, four other publications: a weekly, two monthlies and a cultural magazine.

The second category comprises those publications published in France for a foreign readership: they will be either the small publications of political refugees or newspapers published by minority groups. These will be dealt with at greater length below in the section on the flourishing of minority papers. But skimming through what is published in Paris, one finds a surprisingly rich harvest of periodicals published by tiny groups, from the *Revue des Juifs originaires de Djerba* (Review of the Djerban Jews) to the *Indian Times* published by the Franco-Amerindian Centre in Paris. Some of the oldest communities maintain their press in spite of their linguistic assimilation. Thus Yiddish papers are still published, e.g. *Naïe, Presse* (communist) and *Undzer Wort* (Zionist). This is also the case of the Armenians: *Haratch*, started in Paris in 1924, still appears as a daily paper. Surprisingly, the largest communities are not automatically in the forefront of the written press. The Italians, Portuguese and Spaniards have given up almost all journalistic activity. And whilst the Afro-Caribbean community in the Paris region is about 500,000 strong, they only have one journal, *France-Iles* (France-Islands), an offshoot of the *Association pour le rayonnement de l'identité culturelle des Français d'outre-mer* (Society for the extension of the cultural identity of French citizens overseas).

To give a clearer picture of this second category of publications, it seems preferable to deal successively with three world regions: Africa, Latin America and Eastern Europe.

Africa

What paper is available for the 500,000 Algerians, Moroccans and Tunisians recorded in the 1982 census? *Sans frontières* (No frontiers) in 1979, followed by *Baccara* in 1986, were born out of a first wave of unrest in the suburbs of large cities. The 1990 rappers may even give birth to a new journalism.

After Bamako, Montreuil in Paris is the second largest Soninke-speaking town in the world. *Sooninkara* (In Soninke country) – 1000 copies on 20 pages with a few pictures – is the only journal of an African community in Paris at the present time. Yet 150,000 Africans live in the Île de France (the wider Paris region). Of course there are such papers as *Jeune Afrique* magazine, or *Amina*, or again *Afrique-Asie*, but these are intended first and foremost, and actually exported to, the countries of Africa. *Sooninkara* is a completely bilingual paper. Indeed, when the Soninke farmers from the Sahel arrive in France, they are often illiterate in French as well as in their native tongue, a traditionally oral language. The first handbook in Soninke was published in 1973. Thus they usually learn to read and write in both languages simultaneously. *Sooninkara* was started in 1988 by Yacouba Diagana with the *Association pour la promotion de la culture Soninke* (Association for the promotion of Soninke culture). It should be remembered, however, that the African press has a long history in Paris. As early as the 1920s, *Continents* or *La voix des nègres* (The Voice of the Negroes) were regular defenders of Jazz music.

Latin America

This continent is represented by *Sol a Sol*, a paper appearing in 40,000 copies and delivered to all South American cultural centres in Paris. It was started by Guadalupe Bocanegra from Mexico.

Eastern Europe

An East-West link review, *Lettre internationale*, has enabled over the last ten years a number of intellectuals from Eastern Europe to be read in the West where they were little known. *La pensée russe* (Russian thought), a journal created in the 1920s, is still published as a weekly, and has still got quite a following. The Polish review *Kultura*, started by Jerzy Gedroye, has enabled its creator to set up a publishing house and be the first to publish Gombrowicz and Milosz .

The minority broadcasting media

One should not forget that the written press is only one dimension of the media. Attempts by minorities to become owners of radio or television stations moved at a much slower pace, due mainly to the heavy financial investment called for. Minority groups in the last few years have put heavy pressure on the media, claiming the right to play a more significant role by increasing the number of minority professionals and ridding the media of distorted group stereotypes.

Since 1981, about 30 community radio stations – African or Asian, Polish or Portuguese – have been started, including the following:

Lyons: *Arménie*; *Pluriel* (Plural – multi-community); *Trait d'Union* (Hyphen–multi-community).

Marseilles: *Beur FM* (North African immigrants); *Diva* (Italian); *Galère* (Galley – multicultural); *Gazelle* (multi-community); Soleil (Sun).

Paris: *Alfa et Portugal FM; Asie; AYP* (Armenian); *Berbère Tiwizzi; Beur; France-Maghreb; Orient; RDH* (Solidarnosc); *Soleil* (Sun – North African); *Tabala* (African and Afro-Caribbean).

All of these stations have an advantage over other private radios in that they enjoy the active support of their listeners. Like other radios run by associations, they are managed by volunteers with varying degrees of competence, often in rundown premises, and are of variable sound quality. Yet the strength of these unusual stations lies in their ability to acquire funding wherever it can be found, and notably in listeners' pockets. For example, thanks to their clubs, charity functions and even 'telethons', *Radio Arménie* and *Radio Asie* once managed to collect almost £10,000 in small cheques.

The recently authorized advertising on associations' private radio stations is still limited (an annual turnover of £10,000 to £15,000 on average). Community radios use it cautiously, fearing the loss of their 'soul' or at least their independence. The advertising turnover of *Radio Asie*, which is run collectively by a number of communities (including Chinese, Kampucheans, Laos and Vietnamese), dropped very suddenly by 50 per cent in 1990. 'It was because, asserted Michel Lefèvre, the radio's director, we told the truth about Tiananmen Square and broadcast reports on the Golden Triangle mafiosi'.

Yet French society needs these community radios. In crisis situations, they play a buffer role and provide a forum for debate.

Two public organizations help them financially: the *Fonds d'action sociale* (FAS – Social action fund) for immigrant workers and their families, itself financed from the *Caisse d'allocations familiales* (CAF child benefit fund); and the *Fonds d'aide à l'expression radiophonique* (Broadcasting assistance fund) financed by a levy collected from the advertising revenues of commercial radios. Both of these public organizations help some thirty radio stations. FAS holds that, if it is to help integration, it has to broadcast in French. On *France-Maghreb* and *Radio Beur*, long regarded as model stations, 90 per cent of broadcasting is in French. This is almost a must, since many listeners only speak French. *Radio Soleil*, however, uses Arabic somewhat more (40 per cent). On the Franco-Maghreb radios today, listeners confide their problems and expect to receive answers to these. *Radios Alfa, Asie, Beur, Gazelle, Soleil* and *Trait d'Union* invite legal advisers or social workers to help their listeners.

As to the input of minorities on the national television network, it is rather slight. The *Association rencontres audiovisuelles* (*ARA* – Audio-visual encounters association) was founded on 3 January 1990 under the aegis of FAS and the *Direction des populations et migrations* (Department of populations and migrations, attached to the Ministry of Labour). It operates as a collective structure, playing an advisory management and expertise role on behalf of FAS for its involvement in the communication field in general and the audio-visual field in particular. Set up for a term of three years, its goal is to stand for 'the idea of a multi-coloured communicating France, like the parrot of the same name'. Its director, Edouard Pellet, is fighting very hard to develop a 'professional tool' that can be efficient in the audio-visual field. ARA is at work in three television programmes. *Rencontres* (Encounters), broadcast on Saturdays from 2 to 8 p. m., aims at facilitating exchanges between people living in France, whether French or immigrants. *Relais* (Relay) a programme for children which is part of *Shama Dynamite,* a Wednesday morning programme, takes advantage of the government-sponsored educational project *Composition française* (French essay). The project's task is to look for foreign contributions to French civilization and culture. Finally, *Racines* (Roots), a documentary programme showing on Fridays from 8.02 to

8.28 am, is part of FR3 Channel's *Continentales* morning news and documentary programme which scans the day's current events.

After producing these three programmes, ARA commissioned the *Centre d'information et d'études sur les migrations internationales* (CIEM – Centre for information and study on international migration) to make a survey of the presence and representation of immigrants and ethnic minorities on French TV. Because ARA's brief was to pilot the activities sponsored by FAS and the ministry responsible for immigrants in the audio-visual field to facilitate the integration of communities of foreign origin, they wanted before completing their task to gain an in-depth view of the French audio-visual landscape in terms of the image it gives of immigrants and ethnic minorities. In so far as the survey was not only concerned with news items, but also fiction, entertainment, games, music programmes, advertising clips and spots (in which visual images play a dominant role), it was necessary to indicate that the survey did not limit its target public to foreigners living in France, but also included French persons of African, Asian or Maghreb origin, and citizens of overseas departments and territories whose 'visibility' sets them up as an ethnic minority in French society.

The 'subject' or 'person' the survey was concerned with went beyond the legal concept of foreigner or even of immigrant to include, among others, 'Beurs' (persons of Arab descent) and the new generations born of African and Asian immigrants. The survey was intended to check quantitatively the degree to which such subjects had access to the television journalist's profession, were a source of information in the national and international news, were integrated into the realities of current French social and cultural life and were represented in television broadcasts and televised political discussion.

The survey also examined ways of identifying these different elements in the various television channels in order to obtain the clearest possible view of the role played by public channels in comparison to private and commercial ones and the function of the various items (information, sport, fiction and advertising). The survey covered a brief 15-day period from 16 to 30 October 1991. A one-month span of TV production would have been preferable. This is one of the main limits of the survey, although two other problems should be mentioned.

The first of these involves the concept of value representation. From the outset there was confusion between an assessment of the values represented and an assessment of their actual representation. After correction the answers had lost much of their meaning: the journalistic style, where facts take precedent over comment, often obscured the question of value representation. The second problem had to do with advertising: any qualitative analysis of advertising calls for a study of its own.

Some conclusions

A number of conclusions can be drawn from the overall picture of national and international news, some of which are given below.

1. Immigrants have only limited access to television. Professionals of immi-

grant origin are scarce (the names of only three journalists of Maghreb origin appeared in 555 hours of programming). In spite of the politically controversial character of the topic, immigration is clearly not a major news item. Situations relating to it are dealt with only sparsely in the media, and then only in a dramatic way which reflects the obsession of the political class and of public opinion.

2. Immigrants and ethnic minorities are de facto an integral part of French social reality. Consequently it seems that no social movement, or significant social phenomenon, involving industrial urban society or the services sector can be portrayed without the immigrant component being part of the televised image.

3. This image is presented without commentary or elaboration. The negative corollary of this de facto integration into current events coverage lies in a relative medley of images. For example in several reports, which again never mentioned immigration, on the subject of the 'bogus unemployed', the pictures put out by the *Agence nationale pour l'emploi* (National employment agency) showed mostly North Africans and Blacks. In this instance, immigration appears to be a constituent element of a presentation of the unemployment problem.

4. Reporting on problems in urban areas, including security, violence in secondary schools, and the role of the police with their periodic blunders often includes images of immigrants or ethnic minorities. Integration was the main subject of the TV programme on youth entitled *La marche du siècle* (The march of the century) shown on FR3 on 16 October 1991 in which Edgar Morin, analysing youth movements in France over the previous ten years, identified two phases – *SOS Racism* and *Génération chômage* (Unemployed generation) – that featured the action or presence of the new generation born of immigrants.

5. As regards news items, several criminal affairs involving persons of foreign origin were reported with commentary in FR3 regional bulletins. During the period of the survey, these bulletins reported on Chinese immigrants in Paris in connection with a brawl, the discovery of forty-six clandestine workers, the efforts of a neighbourhood association to combat the squalid living conditions of immigrants from Eastern Europe in Central Paris and the break-up of a Chinese network of clandestine workers. Even without commentary, or any reference to the ethnic origin of the immigrants concerned apart from skin colour, the news items none the less play a fundamental role in relaying a certain image of the immigrant populations.

6. Integration, although it is a recurring theme in all commentaries on immigration, is rarely covered in a positive sense in actual reports. Only the performances of stars of foreign origin such as Tahar Ben Jelloun, a writer from Morocco, and Smaïn, a humorist of Algerian origin, on FR3 on 27 October, give a positive image of integration.

91

7. The matter of racism is obviously a matter of capital importance. Several broadcasts were devoted to this theme, although mainly in a European context, as in *Direct* (23 September 1991) about hatred in Europe. Racism in news bulletins was mentioned chiefly in connection with the coverage of the trial of the 1988 attacks on the Sonacotra homes for immigrant male workers. The theme of racism comes out on all channels as a discrete media category which, contextualized within the French tradition of hospitality, confines the immigrants in a role of victims.

8. During the period covered, a significant number of international events, indicating a shared history with the countries of origin of the largest foreign communities in France, were only partially processed and exploited from that point of view by the news bulletins.

The survey gives little room for complacency in regard to the presence of ethnic minority personnel in French TV. Their marginal presence as professionals in front of the camera seems to echo the state of their overall employment in the French TV industry. Certainly television's representation of multi-ethnic France is far from adequate.

Case studies

The Chilean minority in exile

When faced with the fact that they had to interact with other cultures that were ethnically and linguistically different, the reactions of Chilean exiles depended to a great extent on their personal motivations. If exile was lived in a collective way at the outset, in relation to a shared past and with common ideals, the will to struggle against dictatorship and myths that progressively withered away, individuals underwent change without ever ceasing to be themselves. They never forgot, but understood that exile was giving them the opportunity to grow richer by living new adventures.

A new form of communication, the graphic micromedia, allowed this minority to define its identity. Through literary expression and a network of socio-cultural relationships, the printed page acts as a statement to the effect that the vanquished have not been forced into silence.

What are the main features of these micromedia?

The term 'graphic micromedia of the Chilean exile' has been applied to a number of printed papers, newspapers or magazines, which with a circulation of under 2,000 copies (monthly or bi-monthly) serve as a cultural link between the exiled Chilean community and the host community. A number of micromedia limit their information to events or achievements of the Chilean community; others include news and information about the milieu in which they live; bulletins are edited in two languages and interact with creative work of other artistic groups, such as poets, painters, musicians, dancers and so forth.

These marginal papers or magazines are the voices of the Chilean community regrouped around social, cultural, sports and trade union organizations. Their aim is to inform, expose oppression and facilitate integration. One reason why such periodicals are often short-lived is the lack of financial resources. These media live thanks to the voluntary contributions of their supporters, or from the meagre advertising revenues paid by companies or organizations created by the exiles themselves. By and large such periodicals are printed by self-managed technical and administrative units.

Presentation of some of these reviews

La Porte (the Door)

This review has been produced in Paris since May 1985. It differs from other micromedia edited by Chilean exiles. It is bilingual, deals with political, social and cultural themes through the imagery of poetry and fosters links between the Chilean and other communities (Arab, Portuguese, Spanish and others). Moreover, its impact goes beyond graphic communication because it stimulates the creation of cultural groups and organizes meetings and debates on Latin America. The heterogenous character of the review, where many different Latin-American nationalities are brought into contact, breeds intellectual cross-fertilization. At the same time the confrontation of their culture with that of the host country brings the contributors and readers into contact with a single, dominant model. The review is distributed and sold through a network of correspondants and by a number of Parisian bookshops.

The Selso review

This forty-four page review has been published since 1977 under the directorship of the exiled Chilean journalist, Hugo Arellano, and deals with a series of subjects related to the socio-political situation in Latin America. Published in Spanish, the articles are written by contributors living in Chile and other Latin-American countries, or in Europe. After so many years, it may be said that this micromedia meets the need for expression of this minority. A run of 1,000 copies are produced twice monthly by a narrow family circle: it has maintained its economic independence thanks to the support of its editor-publisher.

The information bulletin Central Unica de Trabajadores de Chile

Following the coup in 1973, the *Central Unica de Trabajadores* lost its legal status as the principal trade union of the Chilean workers. Its leaders, whose most fundamental rights were denied, then began co-ordinating via an external committee which for ten years edited a bulletin as a link between workers inside and outside Chile. Its appearance at monthly intervals and its circulation in forty countries give some idea of the responsibility assumed by its editing board under the direction of Luis Alberto Mansilla. Published exclusively in Spanish and lavishly illustrated, its most important articles were devoted to union information, reports and politico-cultural subjects.

When the *Central unica de trabajadores* reappeared in Punta de Tralca in August 1988, it became clear to the leaders of the external committee that the prospects of a return from exile were good and that they could envisage a merger with trade union organizations, and so they decided to return to Chile. The bulletin's objective had been achieved.

The Araucaria review

Araucaria is an exacting unifying instrument in which progressive Chilean intellectuals express themselves, whether they live inside or outside Chile. Edited in France and published in Madrid since 1979, its objectives have expanded in spite of great difficulties. This review is sold and circulated in almost forty countries.

The Tzigane ethnic minority

Presentation

'Tzigane' is the most widely used name in French-speaking countries today for this heterogeneous population, a stateless society without a territory whose members are linked in a very specific manner. In demographic terms, the Tzigane or Gypsy population is quite sizeable. They total more than three million persons scattered in the member countries of the Council of Europe and almost four million in Eastern Europe. The estimates of those living in France vary between 200,000 and 400,000.

Tzigane history features a succession of migrations. They appear to have been first heard of around the tenth century of our era when they left the north-west region of India. It is possible, following linguistic clues, to retrace their migrations which, via Iraq and Armenia, took some of them up to the edge of the Bosporus and to Greek-speaking countries. It is only at the beginning of the fifteenth century that history begins to mention their arrival in Western Europe. The Dutch, English, French, German and Spanish States drew up repressive legislation which drove some of these populations to settle *en masse* in the Iberian Peninsula, for example, while others scattered, or were even expelled from countries such as France and the Netherlands. The first migrations of Tziganes back to France in the course of the nineteenth century came from the German part of Europe. Most of them were Manush or Jenish musicians, peddlers or basket-makers. From the Iberian Peninsula there also came Catalan Gitanos attracted by the fairs of the Midi. But the middle of the nineteenth century was also the theatre of other events in Eastern Europe, for example the phasing out of slavery in Rumania which led to the departure of Rom Kalderash and Tchurara. The first waves reached Belgium, France and Germany in 1866. As early as 1911, another migration began which was to extend worldwide: that of Rom Kalderash originating in Rumania, although culturally transformed by a very long stay in Russia. The Roma from Yugoslavia only appeared in the 1960s and 1970s in search of work. More recently the political upheavals and economic hardships in

Eastern Europe have prompted other Tziganes to move westward. The recent changes in Eastern Europe have had adverse consequences for the Tziganes in two ways: a minority ethnic group with no specific protection from a particular state, they are scapegoated by those who are disappointed by liberalism as well as by those who rediscover exclusive nationalism. Hence the tens of thousands who today are knocking at the Common Market doors.

Relations between the Tzigane minority and the French media

Prejudices against the Tziganes expand ceaselessly through space and time. The stereotypes and prejudices spread by oral tradition have been confirmed by the messages conveyed by the media, reinforced by the technological impact specific to our time. Any effort to obtain a better understanding of the Tzigane reality and a more whole-hearted acknowledgement of their traditional and cultural values should focus first and foremost on the media, particularly on decision-makers.

Up to now the various organizations working with the Tziganes, be it in social or research work, have given scant attention to this media-centred approach. The Tzigane minority has never been at liberty to speak for itself. As a marginalized social group with no means of presenting their own image of themselves, they are forced to accept the image drawn and promoted by a dominant non-Tzigane society. Literature, drama and music have unfailingly conveyed clichés strengthening erroneous ideas about the Tziganes. And the media have now taken over the task, as is well known.

The written press has a strong tendency to focus on certain aspects of Tzigane life at the expense of others which are never mentioned because they do not conform to the accepted image composed by non-Tzigane persons. For example when a representative of the Tzigane world, Matéo Maximoff, received the 'Médaille du mérite artistique' at the Ministère de la Culture, the event was totally ignored, whereas the very same day the press was all too happy to deal at great length with a 'typical Tzigane news item', in other words a brawl in a café in the South of France in the course of which a man died. While the world-wide nature of the media potentially provide social and ethnic minorities with the opportunity to disseminate a true positive image of their way of life, beliefs, customs, crafts and folklore, one has to admit that there is precious little evidence of this as far as the Tziganes are concerned.

Within the realm of audio-visual media, however, one particular experiment deserves all our attention. The Yugoslav regional television for the Kosovo region broadcasts a programme made by the Tziganes themselves. Every Sunday morning for fifteen minutes they speak their language and describe their way of seeing things. The success has been such that the time slot is to be increased to a half-hour, and more importantly the programme will be broadcast on the national network. In so doing, a Tzigane group has shown that an ethnic minority group is able to assume at all levels, intellectual, professional and technical, responsibility for a programme picturing the life of their community. Unfortunately this is still a distant prospect in France. In contrast to Roger Gicquel's excellent programme entitled *Spécial vaga-*

bondages, how many programmes such as *Dressés pour voler* (Trained to steal) have misrepresented this ethnic minority?

The cinema too has always made ample use of things Tzigane, including their music and folklore, yet most of the time only reinforcing the stereotype. This has always been the work of non-Tziganes. What opportunity have Tziganes ever had to create and disseminate their message in this manner? Such an opportunity, however, was seized by Tony Gatlif, a Tzigane actor who wrote and directed the French film *Les Princes* in 1988. In it he showed for the first time how Tziganes view their life.

Existence of independent media for this minority

Associations for the dissemination of Tzigane culture aim directly at public opinion. One of these is the *Union nationale des institutions sociales d'action pour les Tziganes* (UNISAT – National union of Tzigane social service institutions) which helps to produce the *Études tziganes* review, a quarterly review founded in 1955 and officially approved by UNESCO.

UNISAT is officially recognized as a popular education organization. It contributes to the work of the national committee for information and social action for travellers and persons of nomadic origin, from which it took over in 1984. Its policy is one of respect for cultural identities and involves launching and supporting a variety of activities in the economic and social spheres in the matter of settlement, housing and schooling. UNISAT also contributes articles to *Études tziganes*.

Publications of the Centre de recherches tziganes

The Centre de recherches tziganes (Centre for Tzigane research) is an academic body set up in 1974. Its task is to develop and promote research and studies relating to the Tzigane populations and to travellers, and to disseminate their findings by means of publications, teaching and the organization of scientific meetings. Its director is Jean-Pierre Liégeois, a sociologist and professor at the Paris V René Descartes University. Its main publication, *Interface*, is an academic review far removed from the day-to-day life of the Tzigane minority.

Other publications appearing regularly include *Le Monde gitan* (Gypsy world) quarterly which is edited by the *Notre Dame des Gitans* (Our Lady of the Gypsies) association. It publishes articles on Tzigane life at regional level and is very informative. The *Vie et lumière* (Life and light) review is edited by the Tzigane Evangelical Mission and aims to make the Gospel known to the Tzigane people. Several other minor bulletins are published on a fairly regular basis by various associations of travellers' friends such as *Alpha* (Ille et Vilaine) or *Le Voyage* (Rennes). Their chief interest lies in the fact that they provide outlets for Tzigane children and adolescents to express themselves.

Some national or regional papers or magazines occasionally publish articles that take a positive stand in regard to the Tzigane world. Instances include the review by *Le Monde diplomatique* in 1991 of the book *Fragments tziganes*, edited by Hana Sebkova, Edita Zinayova and Milena Hubschmannova. The three short stories by

Slovak Roms are a sublime introduction to a people's culture. *Le Nouvel Observateur* too paid homage that year to the Gypsy Kings when it reported: 'Their flamenco disco makes the planet dance, but Tonino, Nicolos and the others still live in their wagons around Arles and Montpellier. As they did yesteryear, and as they will tomorrow if the whole world grinds to a halt'.

Again in 1991, *La Montagne* reported an exhibition of photographs by Lialia Kuznetsova, a photographer from the former Soviet Union who casts a friendly eye on travellers. Her exhibition bore witness among other things to the more regrettable aspects of the 1970s settlement policy which led to a number of travelling groups living in near-destitution. The event could be viewed as an invitation to travel, besides being a most moving testimony of life in the steppes with its tents and makeshift dwellings. An article entitled 'From Wagons to Caravans' appeared in the same paper the day before. It spoke of the spiritual values anchored in the hearts of Gypsies at an early age and of respect for the patriarchal family structure and the divine word that have bonded this little-known people into a culture proud of its ancestral traditions. This paper carried a further article a little later entitled 'Tziganes too belong to Europe'. It spoke of Hungarian Tziganes paying a visit to their French cousins settled at Maringues in the Puy de Dôme and could be regarded as having a pedagogical dimension in the French political context that is troubled by the problem of minorities.

Some mention should be made of regional radio stations in this regard. *Radio-Fourvières* in Lyons broadcast two hour-long programmes on Christian Tziganes in 1989. *Radio Trait d'Union* produced a series of 30 hour-long musical programmes entitled 'Liszt and the Tzigane world'.

Conclusion

The risk facing a multicultural France is not so much that of the disappearance of its linguistic and cultural heritage – after all, everything is still mediated by French institutions and the French language – as of seeing each community or group fall back on its own inner world and become totally indifferent to other people. To avert this danger, Jack Lang, the French Socialist Minister for Education and Culture at the time, and his advisors conceived the idea of creating a council which, while it had no decision-making authority, yet provided a synod in which those running experiments in cultural co-existence could exchange ideas and experiences. The idea originally was to set up a National Council of Cultures and Languages in France. All cultures active in the country were concerned. A universal nation in terms of the ideas that had contributed to its foundation, France was no less universal now that other languages and cultures were being woven into its fabric.

There were some who denied the value of this approach, condemning an evolution they regarded as fatal. Such reactions came from Left as well as Right. However, the new Council was created by prime-ministerial decree on 23 September 1985. A purely advisory body attached to the Prime Minister who presides over it, the Council is kept informed of all measures taken in respect of regional and community cultures and is mandated to make any proposals it considers appropriate. For the first time Flemish and Polynesians, Alsatians and Basques, Corsicans and Creoles, Ashkenazim and Moslem French, not forgetting the Armenians and Tziganes, were grouped. Whatever the limits imposed on its action, the Council will stand as a symbol. Following its example, a number of town halls have appointed their own minorities commissions. Lyons, for instance, has a Commission for the protection of human rights, presided over by Mr Alain Jakubowitz, the deputy mayor. In 1991, the Commission met to examine the role and place of minorities in Eurocities. Such commissions should be in a position today to enforce recommendation 1067 (1987) adopted by the Parliamentary Assembly of the Council of Europe relating to the cultural dimension of broadcasting in Europe. This recommendation stresses 'the guarantee for local and regional minority languages of their right to make themselves heard on local, regional and national networks'.

Up to now, minority groups in France have managed to make their voice heard only through their own media, and then only when their community was sufficiently organized to finance the necessary structures. Appeals to national or regional media are seldom heard: and when they are, the community concerned must remain alert to make sure that the content of programmes faithfully reflects its culture and values. Yet there can be no doubt that frequent expression of minority interests and cultures in the mainstream media would help to solve very many cultural conflicts and contribute to an understanding of ways of life and attitudes that are too frequently viewed as provocative by an over-standardized society.

II. CHALLENGING CULTURAL RACISM IN FRANCE
Paul Stubbs

These notes should not be read as a definitive account of the role of migrant media in France. They are rather an attempt to discuss some important themes concerning the ways in which migrant media challenge cultural racism; for the purpose, I have prepared a case-study of a Paris-based organization, Agence IM'média, a multi-media agency concerned with immigration and urban cultures. Many of my concerns derive from a very limited acquaintance with the situation in France and, no doubt, shed light more on my own position as a White anti-racist activist in Britain, increasingly pre-occupied with the development of 'Fortress Europe' in and through the construction of a superior White European identity, than on the obverse construction, that of the inferior, alien 'other'. These notes seek, tentatively, to address the voices of the 'other' as central.

The context of silence

What is clear, even to me in my capacity as an 'intellectual tourist' and cultural consumer, is the absence of migrant workers and/or ethnic minority people in mainstream, and so-called alternative, cultural production in France, either as subjects or as objects. Two examples from my most recent visit will suffice.

The first example, called *Manifeste*, was a major exhibition running from June to November 1992 at the *Centre National d'Art et de Culture* Georges Pompidou. Described as 'A look at 30 years' creation, 1960–1990', it purported to offer a unique insight into the best of fine arts, design, mass-produced objects and architecture. In fact what was presented was astonishingly Eurocentric in terms of the choice of artists, writers, musicians and photographers. This was coupled with an unforgivable silence on the racialized economics of the process of creation itself. In the exhibition, creation and style attain the status of autonomous artistic facts, disconnected and unlinked from the processes of their production, underpinned by an exploitative relationship between the First and Third Worlds. The absence of any comment on the use of low-paid ethnic minority workers to produce stylized objects for consumption in the West can only be regarded as racism.

In 1983 Agence IM'média participated in an important exhibition entitled: *Les Enfants de l'Immigration* at the Centre. Nowadays it appears that the Centre is just more hostile territory for those intent on developing a political space challenging cultural racism. Increasingly, radical ethnic minority and Third World art theorists have noted the construction of modernity in 'Modern Art' as White, Eurocentric and individualistic, so that the Centre Georges Pompidou and other key sites tend to construct 'ethnic minority art' in opposition to this being as 'primitive', abstract and spiritual (see *Third Text*, 1991, esp. Checketts, p. 9).

As always, silence is never complete. Consider the work of Ibrahimi M'Bengue, better known as Asse, a Senegal-born artist based in Paris, who has been shown in Paris galleries and had his first British exhibition in London's Hayward Gallery in January 1993. Asse's work challenges Western Modern Art's use of 'African art as raw material, as "animist"/"primitive" symbols to be processed into avant-garde thrills for "sophisticated" Western audiences' (Eshun & Crowley, 1992, p. 16). In the same article, however, Simon Njami, editor of *Revue noire*, the Paris-based review of contemporary African art, wonders about Asse's rise to fame and his possible co-option into the New York commercial art market. Nevertheless, the work of Asse, and other Parisian African artists, deserves wider recognition in France.

The second example, entitled *23 Rencontres internationales de la photographie*, took place at Arles in July and August 1992. The theme of some twenty-two exhibitions was 'The Europeans' since, in the words of the *Rencontres* programme: 'At a time of turbulence when boundaries are being extensively redrawn, what could be more natural than the leading international event highlighting photography's 150 years as part of our cultural history, recording daily events and used as an innovative artistic medium?'

In fact, nothing could be more systematic than the absence of work by ethnic minority and Third World photographers who live and work in Europe and/or whose work concerns Europe. Consider, for example, in Britain, the work of Ingrid Pollard whose photographs 'Pastoral Interludes' place ethnic minority people in the English countryside, thereby subverting particular constructions of Englishness (Maharaj, 1991, pp. 86–87). The collaboration between Rotimi Fani-Kayode and Alex

Hirst has also attracted considerable attention, following the controversy surrounding Mapplethorpe's depiction of ethnic minority male sexuality (Eshun & Crowley, 1992; Hall, 1992). Discussions about ethnic minority photography in a European context could have been inspired by shows based on the work of these or other photographers at the *Rencontres*.

Instead, Marie-Pierre Vincent's photographic journey 'Europe in 150 photographs' is given pride of place, based on one year's travel through the twelve countries of the European community. Set against plain White backdrops, these photographs of 'Europeans in their daily lives' purport to show the cultural diversity of Europe. However, it is a cultural diversity from which ethnic minority people, apart from one photograph of two male Sikh market workers in London, are totally excluded. 'European identity' is thus constructed in ways that deny the ethnic minority presence, much less address the racism of immigration, migrant labour and refugee policies and practices.

Again, photography is central to IM'média's work, based as it is on the agency's origins in training immigrant youth in French cities. 'Everybody knows that young immigrants were stealing cameras and whatever and at the same time they were complaining about their social situation, so we said: "Stop complaining, use the cameras, stolen or not it doesn't matter, to say for yourself what you have to say"' (Abdallah M., cited in Fero, 1990, p. 5).

Now IM'média has a photo section through which a number of ethnic minority photographers are linked with a wide range of newspapers. In addition, photography plays a key role in developing an archive depicting aspects of ethnic minority experience in France.

The debate about anti-racism

The history and contemporary development of the IM'média agency provides a very concrete exploration of current concerns about anti-racist politics in Britain and France. The agency developed as a direct result of an engagement in political struggle around racism in the late 1970s. Participation in these struggles always raised questions of 'information and counter-information', of how to chronicle ethnic minority activism and challenge the silence and distortion of mainstream media. In the process, ethnic minority activists constructed their own subjectivities in forms which also challenged the constructions of the White Left. Hence, IM'média ensured that anti-racism was not defined primarily in White terms (Gilroy, 1988, for an influential critique of anti-racism in Britain on precisely these terms).

This is best exemplified by the experience of 'Rock against Police', a movement launched in France in 1980 to draw attention to police inactivity concerning racist murders and the systematic nature of police repression of migrant youth. The English title derived from 'Rock against Racism' (RAR) although, despite Gilroy's praise of RAR (Gilroy, 1987, p. 117–130; Stubbs, 1987), there were significant, consciously articulated differences. 'Rock against Police' encouraged small-scale, community-based music rather than grand, prestigious, big name concerts in large, remote venues. In addition, 'Rock against Police' was chosen in preference to 'Rock against Racism' in an explicit attempt to counter a victimology discourse along the lines of 'Les pauvres immigrés, faut les protéger, etc.' (Questions Clefs, 1982, p. 53). Agence IM'média grew out of the work of 'Rock against Police' and other types of activism, so that the importance of organic cultural politics was enshrined in its work from the very beginning.

Today the debate goes on with IM'média's powerful critique of SOS Racisme, which has attained a dominant position as a definer of cultural expressions of anti-racism in France. The critique of SOS Racisme is ideological and political. Its discourse is seen, at worst, as reproducing victimology in which White people speak to other Whites about the importance of challenging racism. The slogan '*Touche pas à mon pôte*' ('Hands off my mate') exemplifies this, creating '*les pôtes*' as a new, trendy image to rank alongside '*les Beurs*', and indeed the charismatic Harlem Désir himself, as cultural icons. Politically, SOS Racisme is viewed as an attempt by the Socialist Government to co-opt and control militant Black, particularly Arab youth. SOS Racisme is more of a 'media-built organization than a grass-roots one', according to Mogniss Abdallah, Agence IM'média's director. He acknowledges, however, that there are contradictions and exceptions, marked by the opposition of some SOS Racisme members to the Gulf War, and their involvement in direct action concerning *logements* (inner city housing).

He points out that SOS Racisme was co-founded by the Union of Jewish Students while Arab student organizations were excluded. This was significant in the construction of an anti-racist common sense to the effect that 'our only concern is with the French Republic', so that internationalism, including the Palestinian question, is rendered irrelevant. The internationalist project of IM'média is made extremely difficult in a France where 'self-determination is a crime', and where integration tends to mean assimilation rather than pluralism: ' ... in the end they all agree right and left on the idea of France as one nation, one people' (Abdallah M., in Fero, 1990, p. 12).

IM'média, in its theoretical and political revue of the same name, has also sought to criticize the development of élitism and opportunism in certain sections of the ethnic minority and migrant worker movements in France. The analysis here resembles that of Sivanandan (1985) in Britain, based on a notion that the state is attempting to create a 'new ethnic minority middle class'.

Professionalism and activism

This debate is given very concrete reality in media work. Elsewhere (Stubbs, 1988) I have defined professionalism as a set of economic, political and ideological practices always existing in a complex relationship to the state and to broad questions of hegemony. This is certainly true of issues concerning media professionalism and the role of ethnic minority workers. IM'média, through some ten years of its operation, has encouraged the training of young migrants in the skills and techniques of modern media work. It is not afraid of professional approaches: indeed, the advent of new technology, notably desktop publishing and portable video cameras, is central to its attempts to disseminate counter-hegemonic cultural products.

The politics of media professionalism draws attention to the aims and focus of the work of media organizations. In classic media professionalism the act of creativity is seen as autonomous: expressed most clearly in the assertion that 'I produce what I want to see'. Of course, this is usually something of an ideological delusion in the context of a market economy, the existence of media élites, and so on. Activist media production takes an entirely different stance, seeking to ally its production to the (supposed) needs of particular groups engaged in concrete struggles. This is no less fraught with issues of delusion and, sometimes, production continues to be geared to 'people like themselves'.

Agence IM'média is acutely aware of these dilemmas and contradictions and seeks to produce different materials for different audiences, its guiding principle being that it aims to address the realities of aspects of migrant life in ways that differ from its treatment by mainstream media. This has included attempts to work with mainstream media and their audiences, most notably in its TV work which I discuss below. There have been accusations of 'selling out' as a result of this, although Mogniss Abdallah rejects this since 'This was not all we were doing and, in any case, we knew it would not last forever'. IM'média could not exist, he suggests, without concrete involvement in the grass-roots movements and struggles that feed its work and give it its legitimacy. It is not the case that a generation of ethnic minority activists has now settled on the arena of cultural production instead of other forms of activism. In this sense, then, classic media professionalism is rejected.

Another issue arises when small-scale, activist-led activities expand into larger-scale, complex organizations requiring bureaucratic, managerial and financial structures. IM'média has faced this since, at least, 1989 when TV work boosted its income and staffing considerably, so that salary questions emerged for the first time. At present it has some seven people working full-time with many more working part-time and some continuing to work on a voluntary basis. As Abdallah recognizes: ' ... This situation created a split between those who wanted to continue the militant struggle and other people who were asking for more money' (cited in Fero, 1990, p. 11).

This situation has been compounded as a result of the urban unrest of 1990 and 1991, during which migrant youth targeted mainstream media organizations, attacking camera operators, photographers and journalists. This 'crisis of media legitimacy' has led to some poaching of personnel trained by IM'média; the pull factor of the need to recruit ethnic minority staff finally combining with the ever-present push factor of ethnic minority people keen to use their skills to become salaried professionals in the mainstream media. This tendency towards a new ethnic minority professional media middle class, with an ideology of 'I'm a media professional first and ethnic minority second, third, or nowhere', is less pronounced in France than in Britain and, according to Abdallah, many workers have now realized that they need to have 'a foot in both camps'.

IM'média has attempted to grow while maintaining commitments to activist cultural politics, training and use of the newest professional techniques. This is a delicate balancing act compounded by a partial reliance on funding from FAS, a state-based immigrant social action fund. This has provided a number of loans and some base funding, although overall 'We try to organize now to be able to be self-sufficient. We do not want to be reliant on grants and we never believed that we would exist because of grants' (Mogniss Abdallah cited in Fero, 1990, p. 10).

Television, immigration and *Rencontres*

The relationship between IM'média and the state is exemplified by its television work as co-producer of *Rencontres*, a programme about migration, which was axed at the end of 1991. Even before its axing, changes produced by FAS and the commissioning channel FR3 led to IM'média pulling out, recognizing that, in the shift to the right in French politics, the programme was becoming a propaganda vehicle for the government. There are now no TV programmes for migrants, while many programmes produce distorted images of migrants. As Mogniss Abdallah told me: 'In France we do not have the luxury of the debate about whether specialist or mainstream programming is best: we have neither.' Nevertheless, he does not regret IM'média's involvement with *Rencontres*, noting that there were no archives, nor trained personnel after thirteen years of existence of its predecessor, *Mosaique*, whereas IM'média had trained, or at least given experience to, over 80 people, and used the experience to build up its video work and provide other TV material.

The appalling state of French TV coverage of immigration has not gone unnoticed, having been the subject of a recent conference in Paris (*L'Immigration plutôt mal traitée par la télé: Libération*, 15 June 1992, p. 46). IM'média did not attend because of pressure of work, and Abdallah remains unconvinced of the value of the conference and of a general liberal belief that 'more ethnic minority journalists will solve the problems'. From the *Libération* report, it appears that the conference voiced a simplistic belief in legalistic redress, through codes of conduct, charters and the creation of complaints procedures and an ombudsperson, combined with an astonishing suggestion that France should look to Britain as leading the way in challenging racist stereotypes. The identification of one problem as being that migrants are more 'shown' than 'present' as agents in their own right on French TV is an important one, although it is unclear how far the conference merely reproduced this in its dominant discourse and organizing assumptions.

Unlike television, radio in France is an area where there are a number of stations directed, either mainly or exclusively, at ethnic minority communities. IM'média is not particularly involved in radio work, having a sense that the moment of radio as an adjunct to radical youth cultural politics has passed. In addition, the plethora of radio stations, legal since 1981, tends to be culturally based and to reproduce ethnic competition. However, the importance of such stations to older members of ethnic minority communities should not be understated and is worthy of further investigation. IM'média does produce some programmes and is involved in a new Paris radio station based on a coalition of new social movements, including ecologists, feminists and so on.

Conclusions and current concerns

At the risk of imposing order where none exists, it seems that the range of work currently undertaken by Agence IM'média is based on a coherent analysis of cultural racism and of challenges to it. As a case-study, therefore, it is of immense importance. IM'média's work ranges from the international to the local.

Within France, in the context of a shift to the Right and an emergent populist racism, a number of important arenas of struggle have opened up. One recent project was the campaign against *La Double Peine* (the double punishment) through which those migrants convicted of, in some cases petty, crimes could be deported as well as face punishment in France. IM'média produced a very professional broadsheet chronicling the hunger strike earlier this year which had some success in changing government policy. IM'média has also been active in Hautmont, the French town that voted, in a recent referendum, to oppose the arrival of any more immigrants (*The Guardian*, 30 June 1992). Mogniss Abdallah believes that the populist support for local 'self-organization' poses a greater threat, in many ways, than the activities of the *Front National*, and that IM'média's task is to explain the situation, in the context of an economic depression, to diverse audiences, and to work with migrant youth to tell their story.

Challenging cultural politics raises, of course, the vexed question of culture. 'Expert' academic opinion in France, as in Britain, increasingly poses this question in terms of the role of Islam. Given the Rushdie affair in Britain, this issue has posed problems for radical anti-racism. This seems to be less the case in France where IM'média recognizes the difference between religion as political resistance, representation and rights, and individual belief, in a French State highly intolerant of religious diversity. Throughout its existence, IM'média has sought to chronicle Islamic movements, in France and elsewhere, incorporating class and gender issues in its commitment to democratic and anti-imperialist struggles, most notably in its video *Femmes en Mouvement*, the second in its series on Algeria.

While not abandoning its concern with the Maghreb and with Africa, where it continues to work with local organizations, IM'média not surprisingly is increasingly engaged in activities having a European dimension. As early as 1989 it worked with *GISTI*, a French migrant rights organization, to produce a major text *L'Europe multi-communautaire*, chronicling the development of European-wide institutional racism. IM'média has strong links with other ethnic minority media organizations throughout Europe and is committed to the importance of collaborative working and the development of a European-wide ethnic minority forum. There are links with organizations in Britain including, most recently, a commission from *Critical Eye* for Channel 4.

I sensed some frustration that, thus far, there is a reluctance to commission work other than that which chronicles the situation in France. Scope for genuine collaboration, and cross-fertilization of ideas, has not yet borne fruit. For example, a proposed film about the rise of German racism met with opposition based, Mogniss Abdallah believes, on both guilt and anger. The guilt reaction derived from a recognition that there is virtually no German-led, film record of racism in Germany. The anger was directed at 'foreigners' seeking to explain the very particular case of Germany which, of course, they would not be able to understand. The attitudes expressed appeared to Mogniss to be less anti-foreigner than anti-ethnic minority since IM'média was working with ethnic minority German workers.

As racism increasingly takes cultural forms, the need for organizations challenging cultural racism grows apace. IM'média's diverse work illustrates the possibility of migrant media challenging White definitions of social reality and media professionalism.

References

Checketts, L. (1991): British Art in a Century of Immigration. In: *Third Text*, No. 15, pp. 5–10.

Eshun, K. & Crowley, D. (1992): Rewriting Art History. In: *I-D*, No. 107, pp. 14–16.

Fero, K. (1990): *Agence IM'média: a report on immigrants and media in France*. Migrant Media Collective/Greater London Arts.

Gilroy, R. P. (1987): *There Ain't No Black in the Union Jack*. Hutchinson.

Gilroy, R. P. (1988): *Problems in Anti-Racist Strategy*. Runnymede Trust.

Hall, S. (1992): New Ethnicities. In: J. Donald, A. Rattansi (eds.). *'Race', Culture and Difference*. Sage.

Harris, G. (1990): *The Dark Side of Europe*. Edinburgh, Edinburgh University Press.

Maharaj, S. (1991): The Congo is Flooding the Acropolis: Art in Britain of the Immigrations. In: *Third Text*, No. 15, pp. 77–90.

Questions Clefs (1982): *Jeunes immigrés hors les murs*, No. 2.

Schnapper, D. (1990): Le Citoyen, les Nations et l'Europe. In: D. Schnapper, H. Mendras. *Six manières d'être européen*. Paris, Editions Gallimard.

Sivanandan, A. (1985): RAT and the Degradation of Black Struggle. In: *Race and Class*, No. 26 (4), pp. 1–33.

Stubbs, P. (1987): Racism and the Left: a new opportunity. In: *Critical Social Policy*, No. 20, pp. 91–97.

Stubbs, P. (1988): *The Reproduction of Racism in State Social Work*, PhD thesis. United Kingdom, University of Bath.

Taguieff, P.-A. (1991): *Face au racisme*. Paris, Editions La Découverte.

Third Tex (1991): *Art and Immigration*. Special Issue, No. 15.

Vaughan, M. (1991): The extreme right in France: 'Lepénisme' or the politics of fear. In: L. Cheles; R. Ferguson; M. Vaughan. *Neo-Fascism in Europe*. London, Longman.

5

The development of local radio and ethnic minority initiatives in Norway

S.I. Ananthakrishnan

Almost everyone is talking about television these days. This has to do with the fact that Europe has been flooded with new television channels as a result of deregulation and satellite communication development.* Radio broadcasting is apparently a less interesting topic. But it, too, has gone through a rather dramatic expansion lately. Above all, this applies to the various forms of local broadcasting that we find in almost every nook and cranny. Throughout the Nordic countries there are strong similarities between the various local broadcasting companies. But there are also big differences, for instance with regard to regulations and financing. Broadcasting seems to be at the centre of a new phase of competition, and this has had its effects on programming as well as the manner in which we listen to broadcasts.

The Norwegian radio environment

There is an enormous range of local broadcasting and community radio in Norway which has regional as well as local broadcasting. The Norwegian Broadcasting Corporation (NRK) has 17 regional channels covering one county each. The 1980s saw a considerable increase in the number of transmissions. NRK also has two nation-wide channels, P1 and P2, and a third one is in the planning stage. In addition to this, there is a vast amount of independent local broadcasting activity. Today over 400 organizations have a license to transmit. The exact amount of transmission time

---

* A. Celsing, *Nordisk Medienytt 1* (newsletter), 1989.

is unknown, but the Ministry of Cultural Affairs estimated the total to be about 700,000 hours a year in 1990.* In Norway, the first attempts in the field of local radio broadcasting were made in 1981–82. Since then, the number of radio stations has increased dramatically, with the activity becoming permanent in 1988.

The first licensing period

The first licensing period ended in September 1984. In 1981 a total of 37 licenses were given for trial projects, and this number was later extended to 50. Licenses were given to organizations, associations, companies and such undertakings as pilot projects in schools, and were concentrated in ten areas of the country. During this period seven licences were given to local television stations, four of which actually started transmission.† No licences were given at the time to newspapers, people in business, nation-wide organizations (except for local branches of national organizations) or private persons. These trial activities were evaluated by three public committees in 1982 and 1983.

The second licensing period

The second trial period lasted from September 1984 to May 1988, when the Local Broadcasting Act came into force. The Storting or Parliament intended that the right to grant licenses should not be used for nation-wide coverage that could undermine the NRK. A total of 436 applications were made for local broadcasting, and 179 for local television; 366 local radio stations were licensed in 98 different regions and 281 were operational in 91 areas; 129 licences were granted for local television in 40 regions. Relatively few such licensees managed to survive. In regard to television, eight regions were permitted to broadcast programmes, four or five of which started operating. The rest of the local televisions were connected to cable networks.‡

The present situation

Licences

A special Community Radio Committee was set up to grant the right to broadcast. Licences are in principle supposed to cover one single local council or municipality, although in certain cases they are granted to cover larger areas. The Local Broadcasting Act came into operation on 1 May 1988 and regulates local radio and television. Local broadcasting requires a licence from the Committee.

The issue of licences

The law rules that licenses can be granted only to users. The Committee has frequently had to follow up cases in which the rules have not been obeyed. It has been

---

* Naerkringkastningsnemda (community radio broadcasting board), 1990: *Arsmelding* (report).
† A. Celsing, op. cit.
‡ Naerkringkastningsnemda, 1990: report for 1988 and 1989.

reiterated that a license cannot be a mere object for sale. Every transfer of a licence, of more than 10 per cent of the shares, must be approved by the Committee. Regarding the transfer of transmission time to other licensees, there have been a number of cases in which the licensee, for some reason, has found it impossible to transmit. The Committee has stressed that each licence must reflect a genuine relationship between the programmes sent and the licensee. Proxy licensing is not allowed, although up to 25 per cent of a licensee's transmission time can be rented or lent out to others for network transmission. Some licence holders especially those with limited resources have had to relinquish their licences.

The distribution of frequency and transmission hours is primarily a question that must be solved locally by the licensees. The Committee settles all disputes, and its decision is final. The apportionment of time on a certain frequency has proved to be a problem in the big cities, especially in cases where there are several licensees competing to send on the same frequency. In such cases licensees must give reasons for their wish to transmit at particular times. Since most licence-holders wish to broadcast during the same hours every day, discussion of the allocation of frequencies and transmission times continues to be a problem. Some representatives of other minority radios fear marginalization if all like-minded radios are allotted the same frequencies. On the other hand, this could provide listeners with a recognizable frequency identity.

How radios are financed

The figures from the 1990 annual report of the Community Radio Committee indicate that about 58 per cent of radios are wholly or partly financed by advertisements. Some 36 per cent of all community radios had an annual income of over 16,000 Kroner. Radios with an advertising income of over 16,000 Kroner must pay a levy of 16 per cent on that income to the community radio fund which was created to maintain a differentiated radio environment in which big radios do not dominate the scene. Over the years the fund's assets have been disbursed to radios with a low potential for income from commercials, radios requiring special technical facilities for transmission and ethnic minority radios. A portion of the fund is also allocated for seminars, projects and training to improve the journalistic and technical quality of transmissions. Other forms of financing include backing from media organizations, such as newspapers, church groups and trade unions. Income is also obtained from 'wireless bingo', and some radio stations receive voluntary donations from their listeners.[*]

Who runs local radios

Many different groups broadcast locally in Norway. Nearly half of these have a general profile and do not represent special interest groups. Permits are now given to schools, local associations, religious, political, sports and humanitarian organiza-

---

[*] Naerkringkastningsnemda, 1991: report for 1990.

tions, companies and unions for this type of broadcasting. Among these are newspapers and other public media, nation-wide organizations that transmit locally, cable companies, local councils and even private persons. Such groups, however, cannot hold a majority of the shares in any association of local broadcasters; most broadcasters are organized as private share-holding companies.

There are certain rules governing programmes which should be produced by licensees with mainly local content. This means that at least 75 per cent of programmes should have local relevance. Whether these rules are strictly adhered to is not known. Some types of local broadcasters may do so more than others. One type, especially represented in rural areas or in very small places, usually have their roots in the local community, its people, associations and local authorities. Stations like these broadcast a lot of local news, for instance, direct transmissions from political meetings or cultural events. There can be discussions with local politicians and a lot of direct contact with listeners taking part in 'wireless bingo' or calling to give an item of news. Other radio stations run, for instance, by associations of various kinds may transmit more specialized programmes aimed at comparatively limited groups of listeners such as ethnic minorities. There are also stations of an entirely commercial type, run for business purposes only.

Radio listeners

Inquiries show that 10 per cent of people in Norway listen daily to their own local programmes. Listening varies with districts and age groups. In certain places as much as 30 per cent of the population listen daily. It is mostly young people who listen to local broadcasting. The Oslo station 'Radio 1' is immensely popular and reaches 61 per cent of the age group 15 to 34 years.[*] Indeed, Oslo has one of the largest radio listening populations (72 per cent) in the country. The Association of Community Radios[†] reports that in the Oslo area NRK's programme 2 has 24 per cent penetration. While bigger community radios[‡] have regular listener surveys, ethnic minority radios apparently cannot afford to join the surveys conducted by opinion poll institutes.

Recent developments

The Norwegian national TV Channel 1 and national radio transmissions are state controlled, whereas all newspapers, periodicals and the rest of the media are privately owned. Many of the contenders for the forthcoming Norwegian (commercial) TV Channel 2 are from major newspaper houses and industrial interests. The philosophy of letting market forces decide seems to detract from the decentralized, local character of community radios. This trend is in fact acknowledged by the authorities who are trying to prevent further concentration of local radios in the hands of purely commercial or mainstream media conglomerates.

---

[*] A. Celsing, op. cit.
[†] Interview with the Association's Chairperson, L. Bruusgaard.
[‡] Information provided by the Norwegian Association of Community Radios.

About 424 local radio stations have been given licences, and at least 250 of these are in operation. Two thousand people are gainfully employed in this section, with over ten thousand media and technical personnel at work on a voluntary basis for the community radios.* Over the past few years the character of the community radios has gradually changed. Many of them are transformed into more or less national or regional radios, either through networking with similar radios or by being partly taken over by powerful media or industrial or advertising establishments. The three major media industrial concerns that are actively interested in gaining control of the community radio sector are the Orkla Group (which also owns the major daily newspapers *Dagbladet* and *Bergens Tidende*), the Schibated Group (which owns two of the largest dailies, *Aftenposten* and *Verdens Gang*), and the Aller Concern (which owns all the major weeklies). The latter already owns Radio Network News and has considerable interest in nine local radios in Oslo, Bergen, Trondheim and Stavanger.†

One of the government's intentions in facilitating community radio broadcasting was to prevent media concentration that would compete with the state channels. As explained earlier, the laws pertaining to ownership structure were to prevent large financial interests from dominating the local radios. A very recent study,‡ however, indicates that there are many ways of circumventing the regulations. One of the ways in which this is done is by providing syndicated news and features. For example, one of the big media industry groups has agreements with 125 radio stations to transmit the group's news spots known as Radio Network News. The radios in turn, in lieu of payment for the news they get, transmit advertisements for the advertising company owned by a media industry conglomerate. The smaller radios that are unable to transmit Radio Network News regularly (due to limited transmission time) cannot be part of this deal. Other advertisers are also mainly interested in those local radios that have frequent daily transmissions and a large number of listeners. This makes it virtually impossible for the smaller radios to earn an income from advertisements.

A noteworthy and most interesting aspect of community radios that was not foreseen is that their transmissions sometimes reach audiences far beyond the borders, not only of the community, but of the country as well. Since it is possible to send local radio transmissions via satellite, Russian language transmissions from Oslo and the Far North were beamed to Russia during the failed coup in August 1991. These news transmissions reached thousands of people there thus gaining in importance even though the number of Russian language listeners in Norway is very small.

Another significant role of the neighbourhood radio is that while NRK's national channels do not respond to the immediate needs of each local community, the community radios are able to provide up-to-date information, especially in times of disasters and catastrophes. During the recent cyclone that hit the west coast of

---

* Information provided by the Norwegian Association of Community Radios.
† R. Hoyer; G. Tonder. *Main ownership structures in the media sector in Norway in March 1992* (in Norwegian), Handelshoyskolen BI (school of economics), 1992.
‡ Ibid.

Norway, many people in remote areas received accurate information from their local radio station as to the situation and when they could expect the electricity and water supplies to be restored. Those radios also provided people with important information regarding security measures and emergency help.

No research reports are available on the content of local radio programmes. However, it would be right to assume that radios, especially those with a commercial profile, base most of their programmes on light music to attract a maximum number of listeners. NRK Radio transmits more politically and socially relevant programmes than its counterparts in Western Europe. Many local radios have a similar profile, but a government report observes[*] that, as of today, it is difficult to foresee whether this tendency will continue or is just transient, and questions whether local radio is on the way to becoming commercial and entertainment radio. That will depend on the extent to which the non-commercial section of community radios continues to enjoy a sustainable existence.

Such developments indicate that there are two main conflicting or competing interests in operation in the local radio arena: (i) the socio-political perspective in which community radios are seen as an important decentralized medium for free communication in a democratic society (i.e. the purpose for which they were intended), and (ii) the possibility for the market economy to turn this media effectively into a profit-making industry.

In spite of regulations, the industry has managed to enter the community radio scene. When broadcasting becomes business, and the economic interests override the cultural or social priorities, the strongest and most clever will survive. This development, however, may not have great consequences for minority group radios, as long as official grants continue.

As media researcher Professor Helge Oste put it: 'The media should never be regarded as industries like ice-cream factories, but as a means of meeting the democratic and cultural needs of society'.[†]

Race relations in Norway

In order to understand the context in which the minority groups operate in the media sector, it is important to comprehend the race relations situation in Norway. Norway has a population of nearly 4.3 million. Of these, some 3.4 per cent or about 145,181 are foreign citizens, the majority of them from Western Europe and North America. About 45,000 come from the Third World. The major groups among the latter are from Pakistan (11,500), Viet Nam (7,000), Iran (6,300), Sri Lanka (5,500), Turkey (5,451) and Chile (5,444).[‡] Since the ban on immigration in 1975, the

---

[*] *Ends and means in press policy* (in Norwegian), Statens forvaltningstjeneste (state report), NOU, 1992, p. 14.

[†] H. Ostbye, *Nordisk Medienytt*, March 1992.

[‡] Data provided by the Central Bureau of Statistics, 1 July 1991.

Norwegian Government has pursued a policy of increased control of immigration from the Third World.

Despite the fact that labour migration from the Third World has virtually halted, strong measures are used to restrict even rightful admission of family members, students, visitors and asylum seekers. The immigration control procedures for certain nationalities such as Pakistanis, Sri Lankan, Turkish and some of the East African countries have shifted from Norwegian soil to the countries concerned. Applications for entry are now screened by Norwegian immigration officials with diplomatic status in those countries. This British-style screening procedure very often puts an additional onus on applicants to prove that they have no intention of seeking employment in Norway or burdening the Norwegian social welfare system. Even immigrants who have become Norwegian citizens do not in fact have an automatic right to have family visits or to receive relatives to live with them in Norway. As regards asylum seekers, government representatives collect information about them from the country they are fleeing from.

The revised Aliens Act was passed by Parliament (Stortinget) in January 1991. Many legal experts express the view that the new act is more stringent than the previous one.[*] It does not for example grant children the right to be reunited with their parents in cases in which either party is the asylum seeker. The need for confidentiality regarding information on immigrants or refugees between state institutions such as the social office and the police is not recognized; and the police, social office or health authorities can exchange information that may be considered sensitive by individuals. The asylum seekers' rooms, for example, can be inspected by the police at any time. The reception officers for asylum seekers are even asked, by order of the police, to pack the belongings of asylum seekers facing deportation.

The revised Aliens Act is even stricter following a change recently adopted in Parliament. It authorizes the taking of fingerprints and photographs of all foreigners and in cases of unsure identity, the imprisonment of foreigners for up to twelve weeks. The change went through Parliament in record time despite strong protests from immigrant organizations, human rights groups and legal experts. The proposal was mooted by the Ministry of Justice in May of this year and adopted the following month. This act establishes a direct link with the criminal code. Failure to comply with the Aliens Act as the authorities wish exposes persons to treatment as criminal offenders at any given time.

The changes were in fact proposed by an extreme right-wing party (the Progress Party) as part of a package for reducing and controlling the entry of Black persons into Norway. Over the past few years, and especially since the last general elections, the Social Democrats (Labour Party) and Conservatives have moved more and more into line with the Progress Party's demands for greater control. Many have attributed the Progress Party's gains in the last general elections to its anti-immigrant

---

[*] I. Aguilar, *Samora*, No. 3, 1992.

programme. And the Labour Party has been trying to outflank it by going even further in the race relations debate.

This new kind of backlash, owing to the strict Norwegian State policy towards refugees, has pushed ethnic minority groups into a corner and forced them to take a defensive strategy. The upshot has been to transform refugees into social welfare clients and a burden on any local community into which they have been randomly thrown.* The parties of both left and right admit that this kind of integration policy is a failure but neither of them has come up with a solution. The main beneficiaries of the situation are the right-wing parties and the right wing of the leftist parties. People used to believe that social institutions such as the bureaucracy and the media would have meaningful interaction with minority groups, yet the latter are heard nowadays only when the media or the authorities wish to hear them. Even such words as 'racism' and 'anti-racism' have become problematic. Some anti-racist and left-wing groups should share the blame for this. Once upon a time they attributed all the problems faced by Black communities to racism. The situation now is that all racist and anti-racist groups are regarded as extreme groups in the political media debate. The media are now seeking Black persons who are willing to say that the problem of racism is exaggerated in Norway and that immigrants should learn how to behave in Norwegian society. The media have also become less and less critical of government information, and very often the state's points of view on race relations are accepted uncritically.

Ottar Brox,† a sociologist and politician from the Socialist Left Party, has applied the theory of polarized social debate to race relations. In his book, '*Jeg er ikke rasist, men ...*' (I am not a racist, but ...), he shows that, in a polarized debate, the two parties confront one another with unreasonable arguments, and thereby prevent fair opinions from being voiced. Brox calls it competition of expression, where the two sides compete to be most vocal, whether for or against immigration. This debate, according to Brox, allows no room for intermediate positions. This mechanism of schism-creation is in stark contrast to a critical public sphere in which everyone can express themselves freely and the best argument wins. While he makes an interesting point by comparing articles mainly from a left-wing daily, '*Klassekampen*', with leaflets published by a racist organization called FMI, he does not show why the minorities' own voices are not being heard. Nor has he taken issue with the role of the state in influencing public opinion. Critics of Brox feel that his line of argument will lead to an oversimplified view that equates all anti-racist initiatives with racist ones.‡

As the debate continues over how far or how quickly ethnic minorities should integrate themselves in Norway, anthropologist Thomas Hylland Eriksen§ has recently proposed a prescription for peaceful coexistence between immigrants and

---

* K. Salimi, *Race and Class*, No. 3, 1991.
† O. Brox, *Jeg Er ikke rasist, men...*, Gyldendal, 1991.
‡ H. Lunde, *Samora*, No. 5, 1991.
§ T. H. Eriksen, *Veien til et mer eksotisk Norge*, Ad Notam Forlag, 1991.

natives. In his book, '*The way to a more exotic Norway*', he appeals for the acceptance of Norway as a multicultural society, whether one likes it or not. He extols the benefits of living in ghettos. Ghettos provide the possibility of maintaining cultural identity and surviving the ideology of assimilation. It should be said that the book does not provide concrete solutions to problems of cultural coexistence. In a way it tries to defend the different communities' attempts to maintain their identity.

The rise of organized racist groups and groups with Nazi affiliations has attracted quite a lot of attention in Norway. Anti-racist groups coordinated by the Anti-Racist Centre have recently carried out successful peaceful mobilization against racist demonstrations. The media in the beginning tried to project the organized racist groups as a formidable force, and the discussion on racism centred mainly around their activities. It is important to inform the public about and to contain organized racist groups which very often quote statements and statistics from official sources to justify their standpoint.

The law against the spreading of racist ideas in Norway could be said to be dormant, although the Attorney-General recently stated that violence inflicted with racist motives would be punished.[*]

None the less, racist propaganda can still prevail under the hood of the right to freedom of speech. Anti-racist groups have long sought to obtain a stricter interpretation of the law so that racist expression could be given similar treatment to sexually discriminatory views or information affecting national security. According to Gro Nystuen, a legal expert, there was a clear increase in the number of acts of violence motivated by racism towards immigrants in Norway during the late 1980s.[†]

Some of the other issues that have not yet come to the forefront of the race relations debate are the state of relations between immigrant groups, conflicts between ethnic and national groups, and gender issues within immigrant communities. The fact that many immigrant groups have strong religious affiliations has been exploited for purposes of gain by immigrant fundamentalists on the one hand, and extreme right-wing groups on the other.

The welfare state in Norway is facing one of its deepest crises since the Second World War. The architect of the welfare state, i.e. the Labour Party, is failing to respond to the changing situation in the world where market fundamentalism is becoming a new religion. Thus it easily falls prey to populist and anti-egalitarian measures. Immigrants and weaker sections of society are being used as test cases to try out measures for the infringement of social rights. Public outcry is followed by retreat or entrenchment, depending on the degree of opposition or support.

Whether one calls it pan-European or common European identity, all the talk about illegal immigrants or the saturation levels of refugee intake have all of a sudden disappeared, at least when it comes to refugees from Eastern Europe. Norway im-

---

[*] T. Horn, *Samora*, No. 3, 1992.

[†] G. Nystuen, *Rett mot rett*, Antirasistisk Senter, 1991.

posed visa regulations for North Africans on the grounds that there were fears of uncontrolled immigration from there. On the other hand, visa regulations for people from Poland have been lifted. They can now come as tourists and work here for three months.

The Ministry of Local Government is responsible for making the policy on race relations. In May 1992, a publication appeared under the title: 'Action plan against racism and ethnic discrimination'.* As commented by Ragnar Naess in *Samora* magazine,† this document is an important piece of glasnost. For the first time an official document raises the question of institutional racism. Previous documents had suppressed or given little attention to such racism in Norway. The problem, however, with the document is that it fiddles around with the definition of what racism and discrimination are and attempts to keep the two concepts apart. It defines racism as an ideology that encourages negative discriminatory treatment of individuals or groups based on their racial origins in a broad sense (i.e. language, culture, history and so on), whereas discrimination is described as a negative attitude based, not on racist ideology, but on prejudice and ignorance. The document in other words tries to give a milder definition of persons who are unaware of their discriminatory attitudes and actions. The point is, however, that unless people are made aware of what they are doing, and what the results are for other people, combating racist practice will remain futile.

Such definitions do not help very much in understanding institutional racist practice or racism in, for instance, the allocation of houses. The document's shortcoming is its failure to recognize that Norwegian institutions may practise racism towards the few, while at the same time being accessible to the many. The document suggests the need for indicators with which to judge ethnic discrimination. While education and the labour market are mentioned as areas needing indicators, no such mention is made of race relations policy or minority policy.

In this complex field of race relations, many actors are involved in formulating strategies. Immigrant groups by and large are paralysed by lack of coordination and by internal conflicts. Poor intra- and inter-ethnic communication thus narrows the possibilities for forward thinking. There are some two hundred immigrant organizations, including about forty Pakistani organizations alone, and individual minority leaders often seek exposure and recognition while sacrificing broader group interests. It is now almost a fashion among some of the Black leaders in Norway to sing the praises of the authorities and groups that place the blame for the present state of affairs on immigrants alone. For the majority of the members of ethnic minority communities in Norway, race relations policies will continue to be formulated and dictated by actors outside their realm.

---

* Kommunaldepartementet, *Handlingsplan mot rasisme og etnisk diskriminering*, 1992.

† R. Naess, *Samora*, No. 3, 1992.

Community radios and ethnic minorities

The deregulation of radio broadcasting has opened the way for minority communities to start their own radio stations in different languages. While many radio stations broadcast in ethnic minority languages, very few of them can be considered as owned and operated solely by community initiatives. This as a rule applies as much to immigrant radio stations as to stations in the Sami language, the language of the indigenous minority. The Norwegian Association of Community Radios (Norsk naer-radio-forbund), as well as the Community Radio Committee (Naerkringkastning-snemda), an official body that functions as an inspectorate and arbitration body, point out that exact information as to how many radios transmit programmes in ethnic minority languages is not available. Even the Directory of Community Radios[*] does not have such information. However, it would be right to assume that some of the radios in Bergen, Kristiansand, Oslo, Stavanger and Trondheim where immigrants and refugees live have ethnic language broadcasts, if not independently, at least as part of Norwegian radio stations. The counties in the North as well as Oslo have community radios for the Samis. A few of the Norwegian Christian radio organizations also transmit programmes in some ethnic minority languages. Religious leaders among the immigrants too have become increasingly active in local radio and TV broadcasting. The Islamic Ahmaddhya community has its own radio transmissions in Oslo, as well as some cable TV transmissions.

Oslo, the capital of Norway with approximately half a million inhabitants, has more immigrants, refugees and Samis than any other municipality in the country. The level of media involvement among ethnic minority groups is thus relatively high. Hence it was considered appropriate to study community radio projects in Oslo. Two radios transmit in more than one minority language, and four stations have single minority language transmission. Two stations transmit in Sami. In the following pages two case-studies are presented, i.e. an immigrant radio and a Sami radio, both of which are based in Oslo.

Radio Immigranten (Radio Tellus)

Radio Immigranten commenced transmissions in 1983 and broadcasts in nine languages, i.e. Chinese, English, Kurdish, Norwegian (youth programme), Spanish, Tamil, Turkish, Urdu and Vietnamese. It is run with the aid of about fifty volunteers, a quarter of whom are women. This number includes a few Norwegians. The station has no paid staff. At present a conscientious objector is doing his national service there as an administrator.

Transmissions are for eleven hours per week on the FM-101.1 (stereo) waveband. The radio received financial support to the amount of 150,000 Kroner in 1991, but receives no income from commercial advertising.

Radio Immigranten was the first community radio for and by immigrants in

---

[*] *Narradiokatalogen*, 1992.

Norway. It started in 1983 with absolute minimum expertise, in terms both of technical capability and of programme-making.* Initial transmissions were broadcast from a basement studio shared with the feminist radio RadiOrakel and Kulturradioen, later Radio 1, both of which have become high profile radios over the years, thanks to their ability to win advertising and, in the case of RadiOrakel, support from active women's groups. Like many other radios, access to majority listeners (due to the obvious fact that transmissions are in Norwegian) is an important factor in obtaining sponsors and advertisements.

Volunteers run the radio

Each programme division/language group at Radio Immigranten is expected to have its own technician. Voluntary involvement is a strength as well as a weakness for the existence of the radio: a strength because highly motivated people without any expectations of a monetary reward produce programmes involving the community, thereby attracting listeners from among the immigrant population, and a weakness because the absence of paid employment results in a high turnover of people.

Structure and profile

Each language group is quite independent, and therefore relatively free to choose the content and type of programme it wishes to transmit at any one time. However there are joint editorial meetings once a month to establish a common structure for all the different language transmissions by reviewing the previous month's programmes and planning the month ahead. But the lack of continuity in the work-force, and consequent changing programme profiles, have become serious problems for the radio and call for continuous training programmes for newcomers.

The recruitment policy is based on interest and insight into ethnic minority questions as well as knowledge of Norwegian society. Motivation for radio work naturally is a prerequisite. Some level of commitment to race relations politics is considered an absolute requirement for joining the radio. This political slant is considered necessary by the Anti-Racist Centre which is responsible for running Radio Immigranten. It is also a fact that many volunteers, especially the youth, become politically more aware (in the race relations context) while working for the radio.

It should be mentioned that Radio Immigranten does not have affiliations with any political party or religion. It is a secular radio that is critical of social injustice. It aims at being a link for communication between different ethnic groups. News on topics that are relevant to minority groups is one of the chief ingredients of its programmes and includes news from the Norwegian scene as well as from the countries of origin of the different groups. Important local and world events are covered in all the languages while music and other cultural programmes for each community

---

* S.I. Ananthakrishnan, *Freedom on the air*, India, Economic and Political Weekly, 1987.

are also given priority. Listener interaction is sometimes facilitated through dial-in programmes which are very popular. At election time in Norway and other countries (e.g. in Chile), listeners are very active in expressing their views on the air.

Training necessary

There is no organized training programme for radio volunteers. Volunteers are exposed to learning by doing. Programme production is the main form of training. However, newcomers are normally offered a weekend introduction programme in which they are informed about the structure of the radio, the duties and responsibilities of volunteers, and the race relations context of the radio's existence. In late 1990 an attempt was made to train ethnic minority radio volunteers on the basis of an organized curriculum. But it was not possible due to lack of funds and training facilities. By comparison, it should be noted that the Christian radio network consisting of nearly 200 community stations, and trade-union run or newspaper-controlled radio stations conduct regular training sessions in programme-making and journalistic exercises. This is because they have access to funds. Radio Immigranten is considering the possibility of using such training facilities should funds become available. Even though the Community Radio Committee recognizes[*] the need to improve the standards of local radios through training, the availability of such training is limited. Only the Institute for Journalism in Fredrikstad offers a one-week course for community radio personnel as well as courses in topics such as Minority Issues and Development Journalism for working journalists. However, no courses tailor-made for minority radio personnel are to be found.

Financing

Radio Immigranten received in 1991 about 150,000 Kroner from the Norwegian Community Radio Fund from which a major sum of 80,000 Kroner was deducted to pay for broadcasts and telephone calls, and about 50,000 Kroner for rental of premises. Any outstanding funds are normally used for the purchase of records, news material and replacement of or repairs to equipment. Another source of income is via project financing. Government agencies sometimes finance radio programmes for specific purposes. For example, the Directorate of Health recently expressed an interest in the radio's information programmes on Aids. Information on local elections is another project that has been funded.

Problems and prospects

Running programmes in many languages causes problems of availability of studio space prior to broadcasting. The studio is shared by nine different languages for both production and transmission facilities. This makes the editing and preparation of prerecorded programmes quite difficult and often leads to conflict between the different language groups. It also means that it is quite impossible to expand the

---

[*] Naerkringkastningsnemda, 1991: report for 1990.

transmission spectrum to include other languages. However, following demands from the Finnish group living in Oslo, the radio is planning to provide transmission time for such languages. Several other language groups are also waiting to join Radio Immigranten, including Eritrean, Farsi and Punjabi.

Positive developments include moves on the part of minority radios in other regions of Norway to share programmes. For instance, radios in Trondheim and Bergen use programmes in Tamil produced by Radio Immigranten in Oslo. It is interesting to note that the BBC (foreign language transmissions) was willing to authorize Radio Immigranten to re-transmit some of its programmes including news, educational and entertainment programmes, but this did not prove feasible due to lack of funds to obtain a certain type of satellite receiver.

Views of radio immigranten's programme producers

Discussions with volunteers reveal some interesting observations about the Norwegian media in general, and the role and future of ethnic minority radios. Some volunteers are of the opinion that the majority media are conflict-oriented and inclined to highlight the negative aspects of the Black community.

Mr K. M. Nanda, one of the programme editors, points out that Radio Immigranten plays an important role, however small. As a former employee of Radio Ceylon, he says that the quality of Radio Immigranten programmes may be favourably compared with those of professional radios. It provides the community not only with music and entertainment, but also involves it in the preparation of programmes, while acting as a channel for news and opinions.

The Radio is criticized by some organizations for not being committed exclusively to their point of view. Radio Immigranten is also blamed for sometimes focusing predominantly on the Norwegian situation rather than on the countries of origin of the communities. The contrary opinion is heard too. Nanda adds that criticism is unavoidable, whatever one does. For its part, the majority of the population are indifferent to immigrant language transmissions. Understandably enough, in view of the language barrier.

Besides the Youth programme which goes out in English and Norwegian, Radio Immigranten also tries to provide a few hours of Norwegian transmission because the majority media as a rule do not air the views of the minority communities. In a recent positive development, the students of the Norwegian School of Journalism in Oslo have shown some interest in Norwegian language broadcasting for Radio Immigranten on a regular basis.

Another volunteer at the radio, Mr R. Jeevan, feels that it would be unrealistic to expect the radio to survive on a commercial basis, or to sell itself to a major station and still hope to maintain its independence. With income from commercials, and financial backing from media, business or religious groups, Norwegian stations can afford to have a highly professional style. This attracts many listeners, which in turn brings more advertisements and sponsors, so that journalists and other radio staff can be employed on a full-time basis. Money also provides access to and facilities from mainstream news agencies and entertainment events. Furthermore, the financially stronger community radios can afford a proper administrative infrastructure in order to operate effectively, a feature that Radio Immigranten lacks.

Career opportunities

The independent ethnic minority media sector in its present form does not provide career opportunities, but it does act as a stepping-stone for entry into the media profession either at mainstream level or in minority outfits attached to this, such as the ethnic minority programmes of the Norwegian Broadcasting Corporation (NRK). Radio Immigranten has been a springboard for careers in the mainstream radio and TV media for upwards of ten people in recent years. This applies to Norwegians as well as to immigrants. There is every reason to believe that many volunteers aspire to a career in the media. Some of them have already had media experience in their country of origin, many having left there because of the very fact that they were opposing authoritarian regimes through publications, writing and active campaigning. Also, people with some media background, but who do not have access to other media, come to Radio Immigranten for more experience and leave for paid positions whenever they can.

NRK's Turkish and Urdu transmissions have had occasion to call upon Radio Immigranten's volunteers and offer them jobs for short or long periods. At least two Norwegian volunteers from Radio Immigranten now have full-time employment with NRK Radio. Additionally, one of the Norwegian coordinators at Radio Immigranten now produces regular television programmes for NRK, while a Black woman activist, who was one of the founders of Radio Immigranten, has now become a full-time TV producer for a private company. Having worked at Radio Immigranten is a definite plus for admission to journalist/media schools or jobs with the mainstream media.

Finally, many people who work with the Radio are active in other kinds of cultural activities too, such as theatre and music. Many volunteers say that working at the Radio not only gives them insight into how the media work, but also gives them a lot of self-confidence. For example, the Pakistani volunteers at Radio Immigranten are now actively involved in a theatre group called Azzadi Theatre. This group is currently producing the Norwegian playwright Ibsen's 'Doll's House'. And a Radio youth coordinator from Africa has now set up his own radio station, Radio Knock-Out, and formed a Black theatre group.

Local radio and the Sami community

No discussion of media and minorities in Norway would be complete without an analysis of the media environment in relation to the Samis, an indigenous Norwegian population formerly called Lapps, a term that is no longer used. The Samis are widely dispersed from the counties of Hedmark, Oslo and South Trondelag in the south to the county of Finnmark in the north. Almost half of their number live in the northern provinces. The Census shows that there are about 30,000 Samis in all and that, apart from urban dwellers – many of whom live in Oslo – a very large number live on the land and through fishing. About 10 per cent live as Nomadic Samis, making their living from reindeer husbandry. The rest are teachers, trades-men, white-collar workers and so forth. They do not form a distinct uniform group in terms of livelihood or occupation, and even their language differs from one region to another.

There is ample evidence to show that the Sami communities in Norway, Sweden, Finland and the former Soviet Union have suffered centuries of political, social, economic and cultural oppression. Centuries of Danish colonialism in Norway saw the imposition on the Samis of policies of subjugation and assimilation; they were even forbidden to speak the Sami language at school, let alone use it as a medium of instruction. These assimilationist policies continued until the 1960s.[*] For example, the teaching of the Sami language in schools was not introduced until 1967–68, the reason given being that it was considered a better way to learn Norwegian. It is only recently that the Sami language has been given any independent status, so that studies may be undertaken in Sami as a medium of instruction, even at secondary-school level.

The situation of the Samis became the focus of attention in the late 1970s when the Norwegian Parliament allowed the Government to build a dam in Alta to produce hydroelectric power, which was regarded by many as a threat to their life-style. The Samis won the support of environmentalists and others. A peaceful campaign of civil disobedience was launched to prevent the construction of the dam. However, the campaign did not succeed in changing the policy of the then social-democratic gov-ernment. The latter even called out the army and police to disperse the protesters who chained themselves together on Sami land. Yet one positive fall-out was that the Sami issue was put on the agenda. Another interesting outcome of the protest was that many Samis suddenly came out into the open and revealed their partly hidden identity. They dusted off their Sami costumes and began to wear them with pride. The Alta campaign was the forerunner of a series of reforms. An article on Samis was added to the constitution, the Sami Language Act was introduced and, not least, the Sami Parliament came into existence in 1989.[†] The latter, however, has only an advisory role. In the wake of all this activity, a process of revitalization of Sami language and culture has begun.

The Sami organizations have been able to use the media very effectively in the recent past: for example, their excellent narrative tradition has been put to use in making successful films such as 'Veiviseren' (The Guide), and a documentary in co-operation with the Aborigines of Australia. Another film that gained acclaim was 'The Grouse Shoot' made by Nils Gaup who also directed 'Veiviseren'. His films have been funded mainly by the government, and Sami artists from Finland, Norway and

---

[*] Nordic Lapp Council, *The Lapps Today*, University Publishers, 1969.
[†] M. Lindstad, in *Felleskap til besver*, University Publishers, 1992.

Sweden have acted in them. Sami theatre and singers too are popular among both Samis and Norwegians. One singer also made it to the Eurovision song contest. A Sami professional theatre group called Beyvvas is very active in Finnmark county.

With regard to newspapers, only one is published in the Sami language and is called 'Sami Aigi'. About ten literary books in the Sami language are published every year with support from the government.[*] Only about 2,000 or so Samis can read and write their language which, although very resilient, is spoken fluently only by some sections of the community. On the other hand, in parts of Finnmark there are still some old people (and very young children) who can only speak Sami. A Sami journalist has pointed out that the assimilation process among the Samis is so far advanced that people have chosen to repudiate their origins and question their values. Thanks to the new school system, however, more and more people today are choosing the Sami language as their first language.[†]

Sami Radio

The development of community radios among the Samis should be viewed in the context described above. Some radios operate in the Northern Sami language, but very few of these are run solely by Samis. In some cases they operate as part of local Norwegian radios, such as Radio Forsanger or Radio Alta in Finnmark. Some Christian radio groups in the northern counties transmit in Sami as well as in Norwegian (Radio Doaivuu). Among the few radios run solely by Samis are Guuvdageainnu Lagasradio, Radio Siellan and Radio Ofelas. The latter is run by the Sami 'Oslo Samiid Aser' vi' organization. It may appear strange that a Sami radio is run from Oslo. Yet, as a matter of fact, 8,000 Samis live in the Oslo region, the area with Norway's densest Sami population. Discontinuity in management and lack of volunteers led to a break in transmission in 1991, but it is now back on the air. Radio Ofelas concentrates on news and discussion programmes with Sami culture and music.

Problems of financing

Mr Jan Gunnar Furuly, the radio's chief editor, complained that funds are not available and that they cannot expect support from the Community Radio Fund because of bureaucratic objections at the fact that the application was made a day after the deadline. Radio Ofelas is not a commercial radio but gets modest support from the trade unions and local government, while five or six persons volunteer their support as technicians and journalists.

Radio and politics

Mr Furuly describes the role of the radio chiefly as being a source of information to the Sami community in Oslo. Parts of the broadcasts are in Norwegian, because of the variety of Sami dialects and the fact that years of assimilation mean that many Sami understand Norwegian better than Sami. The radio hopes to pro-

---

[*] Data collected in conversation with Norwegian Council for Culture personnel.
[†] E. Aslaksen, *Finnmarken* newspaper.

mote Sami language and culture by making programmes in co-operation with well-known Sami artists. The political role of the radio was also highlighted by Furuly. He observed that the Sami Parliament can play an effective role if more Samis participate in the election process. In the last election to the parliament, barely 20 per cent participated. This is due mainly to a deep-rooted suspicion of political institutions among the Sami community.* Many are wary of registering themselves as Samis for fear that a Sami register could easily be used by an occupation army against them as happened during the Nazi occupation of Norway in the Second World War. Radio Ofelas intends to dispel such fears and mobilize the Sami population to voice their demands through political participation. However, some people question the validity of the reasons put forward to account for the Samis' low political participation and prefer to link it to the assimilationist policy that has caused so many to hide their identity, while yet others attribute the phenomenon to divergent and sectarian trends among certain Sami organizations. However, the Chairman of the Sami Parliament, Ole Henrik Magga, claims that, unless the Sami Parliament is given real power to manage Sami resources, there will be political disillusionment among the Samis.†

Vicious circle

Mr Furuly works as a journalist for 'Aftenposten', the leading Norwegian daily. As an experienced journalist, he plans to train volunteers to work for the community radio. He feels that lack of appropriate training affects the quality of the programmes, and this in turn reduces the number of listeners. The overall financial situation, lack of training and training personnel, and limited transmission time and facilities feed negatively into one another. 'A formidable task lies ahead, especially as our profile is non-commercial and public-service-oriented', added Mr. Furuly. A similar view was expressed by a journalist from Radio Porsanger. He said that, while many of the radios that have access to money receive additional support from the Community Radio Fund, not enough money is available for minority language radios. 'Even those who come to work for us, later join NRK's minority radio programmes, because we cannot pay them.' Radio Porsanger has transmissions in Kven (the language spoken by a Finnish minority in Norway), Norwegian and Sami. It would appear that long-term involvement with community radios of this kind will not be possible for media personnel unless they are paid as well. The high staff turnover leads to varying degrees of enthusiasm and involvement. Sami language transmissions on the Student Radio in Tromso, a northern city, and Radio Pasvik, which is also in the North, had to be discontinued largely because of lack of personnel.

Future plans for Radio Ofelas

Radio Ofelas has definite plans for the future. Increasing broadcasting hours

---

* Information gathered at a meeting with Oslo Simiid Saer.

† Data collected in conversation with Sami Parliament office staff.

and personnel training will be the main priorities. Lack of administrative skills will be compensated for by recruiting skilled administrators. News and reports from the community will be the main components of the programme profile. The radio hopes to play an active role in connection with the forthcoming elections for the Sami Parliament in 1993. Another area of involvement will be joint programme production with indigenous women's groups in Latin America on issues such as 500 years of European influence since the arrival of Columbus in the Americas. The Samis also recognize the need for greater co-operation with other minority radios such as Radio Immigranten.

'There is a clear need for radios such as ours, but how long can we continue running on volunteerism and enthusiasm without the necessary financial support and training facilities? The trend in local community radios is one of commercialization and concentration. Big media houses control radio networks and even news production. The whole idea of community radio as something controlled by the community and serving the needs of the community may remain an unfulfilled dream if timely intervention is not made by the authorities', concluded Mr Furuly.

People who are familiar with Sami radios[*] point out that such radios in small communities have a better chance of survival despite lack of resources than radios in big cities. In smaller communities there is a lot of interest in creating programmes and a sense of identity between the radio and the community. People from all walks of life there are willing to devote more time to listening and they find radio work more interesting.

Conclusions

Linking the case-studies

Community radios run in many languages by minority groups in Norway are a reality today. Their future development depends on the potential to mobilize financial and human resources and to keep a viable audience. Unlike commercial radios, they see their role as a socio-political one rather than as entertainment-oriented.

There are lots of similarities between immigrant and Sami radios, although there are lots of differences too. As pointed out by A. Hogmo,[†] Samis have a long history in developing their politics. They have succeeded over a period of time in projecting persons and institutions that can work towards achieving political understanding in Norwegian society as a whole. In relation to the Samis, immigrants are newcomers on the scene.

Building alliances is important. Alliances within the immigrant community, and alliances between immigrants and Samis are being discussed more and more these days. However, it should be realized that only politically or culturally active sections have a conscious agenda to build alliances. As minority groups, both Samis

---

[*]   O. Guntvedt, Ministry of Culture.
[†]   A. Hogmo, Enhet og mangfold, En studie av flerkulturelle miljoer i Oslo, Ad Notam Forlag, 1990.

and immigrants are concerned to maintain their cultures in Norwegian society. Many people there have failed to realize that Norway was already a multi-cultural society before the immigrants came. Interestingly enough, some are of the view that immigration to Norway has been an eye-opener and that it has helped the Samis. Máret Sárá, a Sami politician, says that it was only when immigrants came to the country's centre of authority, Oslo, that Norway discovered that it already had a minority. In a sense the Samis have benefited as a result of immigration, not least in connection with issues related to schools and education.*

Community radios are a way of strengthening contacts and co-operation between the two groups. This process must be handled with extreme care and respect for differences in historical and cultural heritage.

Marginalized media, perhaps

Ethnic minority groups are many and fragmented. Linguistic, religious and political diversities do not seem to favour the possibility of finding a strong and unified voice in Oslo. This applies to the media context too. Ethnic minority groups tend to exert some influence only when political parties find them useful as vote banks. They tend to cash in on this by fielding candidates in local elections. The communities in turn put pressure on parties to incorporate issues of interest to them in their party programmes. Right-wing parties, however, recently began to find it more useful to play the nationalist card and blame immigrants for everything from the breakdown of social welfare to the increase in crime.

Norwegian media, as is the case in many other parts of Europe, continue to focus on 'deviant' aspects of minorities. They continuously focus on criminality among minorities and the possible threat they pose to the harmony of Norwegian society's monolithic nature and have virtually made it impossible for anti-racist forces to hold reasonable discussions or dialogue in the majority media. Nor do minority media seem to reach the majority, even when programmes and publications are produced in Norwegian. The Norwegian language programmes and publications brought out by minorities appear to be consumed only by those who are already positively inclined to interact with minorities. The Gulf War and escalating unemployment have further aggravated the negative view of immigrants. It is in this context that Radio Immigranten's activists feel that their role is becoming increasingly important. In order to achieve a broader appeal, it is now in the process of changing its name to Radio Tellus.

Need for financial basis

Two major factors that influence the existence of a neighbourhood/community radio in general are: (a) a secure financial basis for programme production, employment and training of personnel, and (b) a viable audience from among sufficiently large communities.

---

* M. Lindstad, op. cit.

The fragile existence of a minority radio is made even more vulnerable by the powerful commercial radios trying to muscle in on the ethnic radio market. Devoting a few hours to the main minority languages is a common tactic used by some of their number. This enables them to earn a good name while obtaining financial gain through advertisements in minority languages. For example, the recently launched Black youth radio, Radio Knock-Out, is planning to use the facilities of one of the largest radios in Oslo, Radio Oslo. In general the mighty forces of commercial radios and those controlled by Christian organizations, trade unions and other strong interest groups give very little breathing space to small radios such as Radio Immigranten. Some form of financial support from public/government sources is imperative for their survival.

The state's policy of providing support to minority publications and radios through the Community Radio Fund does indeed contribute to the survival of these initiatives. There are not, however, sufficient funds for the employment or training of minority personnel or for professionalizing these radios. It is worth mentioning here that periodicals published in ethnic minority languages or Norwegian publications run by ethnic minority groups are entitled to a subsidy from the government. They have to fulfil a set of conditions including regularity of publication, a minimum circulation of 500 copies and a track record of at least one year. About a dozen magazines receive such support. The total grant however (1 million Kroner per year) is not sufficient to meet the demand. Magazines receiving support are currently published in Farsi, Hindi, Norwegian, Tamil, Turkish, Urdu and Vietnamese. Similarly, in order not to end up with a situation in which only big wealthy radios can survive, the authorities provide funding to smaller radios that have a specific cultural or ethnic profile. In 1990, 8.5 million Kroner were disbursed to 204 radios. This includes sixteen ethnic and linguistic minority groups that were granted a sum of 775,000 Kroner. Many commercial radios have protested against the levy on advertisement income that is used to finance smaller radios, and the Association for Community Radios has asked the government to explore other forms of financing, such as that used to support small minority newspapers.

In the context of inadequate funding, commercial pressures and mainstream media colonization of ethnic minority media personnel, a number of strategies are necessary, one of which should be a more extensive and systematic framework of co-operation. Networks of like-minded community radio stations should be created, not only in Norway, but also covering Europe. The technology is there: all that the different radio organizations have to do is agree on how to do it. The Norwegian Association of Community Radios would support moves to create such networks of like-minded radios.

It is perhaps time to think globally if local radio is to become effective. The presence of immigrant communities interface three realities: local/national, European and Third World. A successful community radio will have to integrate these three aspects while catering for its own neighbourhood.

6

Market forces and the marginalization of Black film and video production in the United Kingdom

Ali Hussein

Introduction

Post-war migration into the United Kingdom was fuelled by a need for labour power, and at a time when other industrially advanced areas of Europe, such as France and West Germany, were recruiting labour from southern Europe, Turkey and Yugoslavia, the United Kingdom turned to the Commonwealth. This was something of a cultural and political reflex and was a contemporary expression of the nation's continuing colonial mentality. Only a few years before, individuals from the West Indies and from the Indian sub-continent had served in the British forces and worked in war production in Britain. For some, this experience of the country influenced their wish to come to work there.

The immigrant communities

One consequence of the role played by immigrant labour in post-war industrial development was that immigrant communities came to be created in highly specific regional and urban locations. This followed from a number of forces operating in shaping the arrival and settlement of the 'coloured immigrant' communities. Primarily the migrant labour came to fill the vacuum in labour from which the indigenous White labour force had fled toward the more attractive new light industries of, for example, electronics and plastics. Hence the migrant labour became disproportionately located in textiles and heavy industry, particularly in the dirty production processes, the service industries and public transport. Since such industries were located in relatively few areas of urban Britain, that is where the migrants settled.

There were, however, additional forces at play. Discrimination in the labour market further constrained the industrial dispersal of migrant labour, and discrimination in housing accentuated their urban concentration. Additionally, a process whereby settled migrants sponsored and facilitated the migration, employment and housing of kin and friends also led to a cumulative concentration of persons from quite specific points of migration. In these processes which shaped the emerging demography of the immigrant population lay the basis for the creation of specific settled ethnic minority communities.

In relation to the communication environment of ethnic minorities in Britain, this is a very important phenomenon. The geographic location of ethnic minorities within specific conurbations, and their further concentration into fairly clearly delimited neighbourhoods within these areas, generated a social *critical mass* which has made possible the creation of a viable sub-cultural infrastructure. Specifically, it has made commercially viable the provision of shops to meet dietary and domestic needs. It has made possible the creation of religious institutions such as Gurudwaras, Mosques and chapels. It has allowed for the use of the community language in the course of shopping, visiting the doctor or seeking professional advice. The presence of a supportive community has provided a platform for collective resistance to personal insult and institutional discrimination. In relation to communication systems, it has facilitated the development of strong inter-personal networks and has made viable the provision and distribution of a minority press. The significant populations which share linguistic and cultural repertoires have also fuelled the emergence of pirate radios, made necessary the minimalist response of local radio to minority needs, and made legitimate the assertion of the commercial viability of further minority broadcast media. When compared to the situation of ethnic minorities which lack such demographic concentration, the importance of this critical mass becomes apparent.

Immigration and politics

The political context within which ethnic minority communities exist has been characterized by a resurgence of xenophobic feeling here and there. In the context of the economic inequity and the political tension existing within the contemporary entity that is the United Kingdom, the invocation of a common 'British identity' represents a useful element in the hegemonic strategy of British government. The 'threat' posed by 'alien' immigrants, the threat of political and cultural usurpation implicit in membership of the European Economic Community and the 'threat' to British territoriality, even in the South Atlantic, have all defined a White British in-group whose interests have been declared to be under threat. There have been equally important threatening elements within Britain, the 'enemy within', which have been defined as including, variously, trade unionists, plebian sectors of the working class and, significantly for this analysis, ethnic minorities. Seidel (1986) has explored the Thatcherite construction of 'Culture, Nation and "Race"', while Troyna (1987) and Murray (1986) have demonstrated how this conception of nationality has been popularized through the British press. The mass media have been a critical vehicle for the successful legitimation of radical economic policies through the effective swamping of opposed views.

Thus it is important that we see British identity as being constantly constructed, revised and repackaged, very often through the media. The communication situation of ethnic minorities is thereby seen to exist within a system of tension that is active and partisan rather than being located within some supposed neutral state which has an unambiguous identity.

Community radio

In the contemporary period of Conservative Party 'deregulatory' policy, we have witnessed a contradictory tension between opening up economic competition within the mass-media industry and an acute anxiety regarding the continued, and even increased, influence over the *content* of the mass media. Thus we have had a new approach on the part of the government to redefine its position as regards the British Broadcasting Corporation (BBC), the introduction of a Broadcasting Standards Council and, for example, a tortuously drawn-out introduction of community radio, which has raised considerable anxieties about the political potential of such broadcasting. Indeed, while the 1988 White Paper *Broadcasting in the Nineties* contained no explicit reference to the communication needs of ethnic minorities, it did show an inclination to regulate the community radio stations. Paragraph 8.4 of the White Paper states that 'Programme operators will be responsible for their own services, subject to requirements ... of taste and decency and of avoiding editorializing and *giving undue prominence to views on religious matters or matters of political or industrial controversy*' [emphasis added].

Presumably the hope was that community radio would offer a more localized version of the bland auditory wallpaper of local radio which caused the Independent Broadcasting Authority (IBA) to express anxiety at the inadequate proportion of 'meaningful speech' to be found in some station schedules (Local Radio Workshop, 1983). Broadcasting policy is a highly sensitive activity in which the state's needs to promote specific economic policies may, unless checked, have unintended and unwelcome consequences in the cultural and political spheres. As Dyson & Humphreys (1985, p. 363) have said, 'Governments that have in the past made a virtue, however implausibly, of having only 'arms length' media policy, in the name of 'freedom of the media', now find themselves having to act as brokers between economic and cultural interests'.

The dominant cultural interests that have been expressed through the Home Office in the last decade have been those of an English/British ethnicity. Thatcherism promoted a populist nationalism that attempted to obscure the internal class and regional conflicts within Britain behind a strident invocation of old imperial glories, complemented by the vociferous identification of alien outsiders and the rehearsal of a racialized nationalism.

Other media

Ethnic minority communities in Britain are well served by an ethnic minority press (Phillips-Eteng, 1988) and are at the same time subject to marginalization and racist reporting in the mainstream press (Murray, 1986; Searle, 1987; van Dijk, 1991). Given the concentrated demography of ethnic minority communities, it might be thought that local radio would be ideally suited to servicing them. However, as one local radio study revealed, 'Linguistic diversity is perceived more as a threat than a challenging responsibility at the local level ... The possibility of receiving information in depth is almost entirely pre-empted by budgetary constraints and scheduling strategies' (Husband & Chouhan, 1985).

The licensing of community radio stations in recent years has added in a limited way to the radio diet of ethnic communities, so that pirate radio continues to provide a rich complement to the official radio. As one commentator has said:

> Black people raid the airwaves every day and broadcast outside the law. Whether they are pumping out music for private profit, trying to bring underground sounds into the open or, like community development radio, genuinely experimenting with the theory and practice of Community Radio, at least they are doing it. Instead of piously offering jam tomorrow, they provide bread today for those who want to hear our music, understand what is going on, or reach the community with serious chat (Odusina, 1988, p. 89).

British television has been criticized over a long period for its stereotypical presentation of ethnic minorities (Hartmann & Husband, 1974; Cohen & Gardner, 1982; Twitchin, 1988). It has provided a capacity to contribute a critical commentary on British racism through occasional documentary and current affairs programmes, whilst more routinely serving as a vehicle for the rehearsal of White British values. Significantly, Britain has a very low penetration of cabling and consequently the importance of this medium for servicing ethnic minority needs is negligible compared with the situation in the Netherlands or the United States of America. The highly visible presence of ethnic minority presenters and newsreaders, and the very few hours of weekly programming for 'Asians' or 'Afro-Caribbeans', does not compensate for the monolithic White English cultural edifice that is British TV.

The Black film and video sector

In this context, as a Black media worker with a long experience of struggle within the British media and arts complex, I wish to report on the crucial significance of the Black independent film and video sector in Britain. For non-British readers the peculiarities of the British use of 'Black' might usefully be defined. Blackness in the British context is used as a collective identity for people of diverse ethnicities who experience a common context of struggle in the face of their experience of White British racism. It is an identity which transcends, rather than denies, ethnic difference.

For many people now working within the media industry, particularly television and associated production areas, the 1990s are set to herald momentous changes in the industry. A steady stream of legislative reforms, re-organizations and new policy inflections are touching every corner of the industry, inducing large shifts in both the cultural and industrial climate with unforeseen outcomes. There have been reforms before, but this time they are coupled with rapid technological changes, and with the impact of legislative reforms that are far more thorough-going than those anticipated when the 1990 Broadcast Act was first mooted. On the employment and production finance fronts, there is enough tangible evidence to unsettle any optimist as to the future of the production sector. Needless to say everything seems to be in a state of transition. This wind of change sweeping the corporate production and broadcast sector will, in time, wreak havoc with an already fund-starved and diminishing independent and workshop production sector. If these omens are not heeded, then key sectors that have played an important role in shaping the cultural and artistic standards of today's television productions will be laid to waste. Far more worrying is the fact that almost all Black film and video production is located within this sector. It is facing extinction and along with it an important cultural achievement nurtured by a vast investment in both human and financial terms.

Any proposal, however modest, that purports to deal with these realities must, for a start, make sense of the plethora of policy changes, as well as attempt to tease out the unspoken imperatives of the political economy of film and video production that are driving these changes towards an open competitive market. Otherwise we will be walking into a future production culture determined solely by market forces. Whatever remains of Black production and cultural values is likely to be a vestigial cultural rump. The question is not only whether a purely market-led production militates against the development of Black film and video production, but also whether this would meet or carry the broad interest of the Black population as consumers with specific cultural needs. It is often forgotten by those who point to the existence of mainstream Black-owned commercial radio stations, a Black cable channel and satellite channels now operating as evidence that the market will take care of every need, that what is precisely at stake is the aspiration of Black producers to engage with popular cultures, as well as with the higher ideals of artistic innovation and experimentation whilst informing, educating and entertaining. It is not an accident that most Black film and video production is located within the independent and workshop sector. Therefore what is at stake is not just Black production culture per se, but knowing what kind of production values will be capable of expression within a mileu defined by market imperatives.

Black art goes independent

The development of a Black production movement in the last two decades in

Britain is inextricably linked to the pattern of settlement of Black communities following the mass migrations from the Commonwealth (Africa, the Caribbean, India and Pakistan) in the period after the Second World War. The scale of this migration and its economic nature has clearly marked it off from any previous Black presence. Firstly, it is a working-class migration in the main. Secondly, race and culture form an important component in the struggle for settlement and constitute the framework through which the Black communities comprehend their relationship with British society, and vice-versa.

It is a population movement of sufficient impact to engender deep and significant changes in the shaping of public policy and the cultural character of the country. It would be simplistic to exclude other factors. It would be correct to say that the Black community's sense of itself and of its culture and above all, its sense of permanent settlement, is born out of the turbulence of the 1950s, 1960s and 1970s and the quest for racial equality and social justice. That struggle was fought on many fronts including housing, trade union rights, the justice system and the courts. The art and cultural establishment started to feel its way toward accommodating Black arts only after Black artists started to organize independently with the emergence of the Caribbean Artists' Movement in the 1960s.

Initially there was resistance to the idea of Black artists working in arts that did not conform to a conception of a European art form, just as there was a tendency to consider as community art all art with explicit social and cultural aims. It was seen as a purely cultural practice and not as art; carnival, dance or literature in the 'nation language' were deemed to perform a limited social function by binding social groups to their heritage, but having no relevance beyond that. They could not, as it were, aspire to the universality and exalted status attained by European art forms. It was a time when any Black person approaching funders for support in no matter what form, whether from the Arts Council or the Regional Arts Associations, would end up in front of the desk of the community arts officer negotiating a grant for their project.

Throughout the 1970s film-makers were working under very difficult circumstances. They were, on the whole, financing their work through a variety of means including digging into their own pockets. Franco Rosso and John La Rose's film 'Mangrove Nine' (1971) and a number of others were made in this way. There were few exceptions. The outstanding difficulties faced by film in the estimation of funders included its sometimes uncompromising attachment and constant grappling with issues of social justice, racism and the re-evaluation and retrieval of much distorted and hidden history. The political nature of such artists' work was a deterrent, and there is no way of knowing how much it was a factor in the lack of interest shown by art funders for the work of Black artists. For many working at the time it was clear that a good deal of political art, agitprop theatre and poster art was acceptable. It was alright for an agitgroup theatre to rant on against employers, but to do so against racism was a different matter. To question notional liberal democracy, or implicitly expose racism, even in the context of a work of art, was deemed to be controversial, alienating, even 'reverse racism'. One Black worker, after exhibiting a piece of work entitled 'For Oluwale' and which was dedicated to a Nigerian who was killed through racist violenece, received a threat of violence.

Black film-making emerges

This was the climate in which many Black British film-makers and artists had to try to find their feet, and indeed, create new and authentic art. There was much to suggest that many Black film-makers were connected to the network of emerging groupings of White film-makers organized around film collectives and groups inspired by the counter-culture movement and other radical stances. There were a handful working in broadcasting institutions or collaborating with White producers on documentaries. Those who struck out on their own had to rely on their ingenuity and inventiveness, either by finding a training opportunity or by starting a production. The mid-1970s saw the growth of several media resource centres in different parts of the country offering training and limited production possibilities. Although such centres were mainly White, many Black video- and film-makers received their first training there. In addition there was a new generation of Blacks who had been through art colleges and were cutting their teeth on small documentaries that had limited appeal; yet they had benefited by placing themselves near these centres where resources for training and production were available.

There was an affinity between the emergent White radical art movement and the development of a coherent Black film and video production practice and culture, particularly in relation to public funding of the arts. Black people working in the mainstream industry were now sufficient in number, with a clear enough profile, to be identified as a group with distinct artistic and cultural preoccupations. In the late 1970s, it was at least strong enough to take advantage of the change in the climate of opinion and of new perspectives developing in art institutions vis-a-vis Black art funding. That process was given a fillip by the watershed events of the civil disorder in the inner cities in 1981 and the soul-searching and re-evaluation of attitudes and policies that followed in their aftermath.

The publication in 1976 of Naseem Khan's report on *The Arts Britain Ignores* opened up the debate on the relationship between art funders and Black artists and art groups. The report did not deal with film or the media directly and no evidence was taken from individual film-makers. Presumably it discounted them because of the way ethnic art was conceived of in the report. It made a number of two- or three-line recommendations, referring only to art broadcasting and provision of information on radio and television. The thinking embodied in the report echoed what many individual Black film-makers felt deeply, along with many art groups working in theatre, dance and the carnival movement, to the effect that the British art establishment was sidestepping its responsibility towards Black art.

The exhortations of Lord Scarman (1982) in his report on the 1981 civil disorders were taken up willy-nilly by all manner of public institutions including art institutions. Various bodies came under public pressure to take up the challenge of searching for evidence of special needs displayed by the Black community in the overall distribution of resources.

In dealing with the period it is noticeable that evidence submitted by the BBC and the IBA to the report skirted the major issues of employment within these institutions. It is symptomatic of the attitudes exhibited at the time to the demands made by Black journalists and artists seeking to enter the industry. The latter did not employ many Black persons, and no contradiction was felt between their responsibility as broadcasters, reflecting the rich mosaic of experience in society, and the lack of personnel from cultural and linguistic minority communities. By and large they continued to rely on either specially drafted Black free-lancers or presenters and journalists from other departments, and particularly the BBC World Service. As for any concerted drive to recruit technicians and production staff, this had to wait for future developments.

Quality first

The BBC argued that it saw no special case for ethnic minority programming since its criteria for programming decisions were based on quality first and foremost. The reason Sammy Davis Jr. or Diana Ross appear on our television screens is that they measure high on the quality scale, not because they are members of an ethnic minority. The BBC believed that programmes such as *Z Cars* and *Softly, Softly* were giving a picture of the contemporary urban environment. It also claimed sensitivity to many of the vocal criticisms of issues of stereotyping and negative representation. However, this was not borne out by the occasional presentation of drama involving Black people or on Black themes. And when the BBC later consented to give Black themes a greater share of air time, it still did not entirely satisfy such criticism. Although, when the new series *Empire Road* was broadcast in 1978, Black people were presented for the first time as protagonists rather than as foils for White characters. However, the series was shown on BBC 2 which is known regrettably as the Channel that nobody watches.

The IBA held that the pressures to satisfy the demands of minorities of all kinds, whether ethnic or not, are enormous and in reality difficult to meet. Its overall obligation, it said, was to 'provide programmes which will be of wide interest, and indeed there is much evidence the existing service does give a great deal of pleasure, stimulation and satisfaction to members of the immigrant communities' (Khan, 1976, p. 156). The IBA was prepared to defend the indefensible. Programmes such as *Love Thy Neighbour* led to a chorus of complaints that the series made a virtue of racial antagonism between Black and White neighbours, or otherwise made it a laughing matter. Yet the IBA claimed that its enquiries showed 'immigrants enjoyed it ... and positively looked forward to it'(ibid., p. 157).

When *The Fosters*, an all-Black family situation comedy series reflecting West Indian life in Britain, was broadcast, it became a landmark. It showed Black people grappling with their own everyday concerns, and as such, for the first time, a TV drama conceded that Black people do have an independent social existence, and a reality other than as mere objects of White hatred or compassion. But despite the advisory role entrusted to a Black social worker from the IBA to work on the script development and production, it bore the hallmark of an adapted American formula barely sustained by the Caribbean flavour given it by some of the actors.

The artistic movement was maturing sufficiently, and there was home-grown talent in plenty, so that there was no justification, even then, not to turn to any of the writers who were proving their talent and ability, particularly in stage drama. Most of them were writing authentic material that was vibrating with the drama of struggles for settlement and fulfilment. The IBA went on to reject the notion of special programming thus:

> Broadcasting is an important factor, but only one factor, in the process of peacefully assimilating immigrant communities into the fabric of British life. So far, Independent Television and Radio have, by and large, avoided special programming for immigrant communities partly because of their obligations to the UK audience as a whole and partly because they do not wish to increase the feeling of isolation and possibly segregation felt by many immigrants. Independent Broadcasting places its hopes in reflecting all aspects of its output, the realities of immigrant life in this country, the contribution which immigrants have to offer and the problems and difficulties which still lie ahead (Khan, 1976, pp. 158–159).

By asserting that they would continue to address the realities of immigrant life, both the BBC and ITV were not saying very much. It was obvious that 'race' was becoming an increasingly dominant issue in the country's political life, due mainly to the growth of Fascist organizations and the rising tide of racial attacks and killings in the cities. The actual reporting of these issues left a lot to be desired. With few exceptions, current affairs programmes usually approach these problems with the aim of understanding the violence and hatred of racists rather than the plight of the victims. Problems of racism were more generally understood within the dominant political framework, as is sometimes the case now with discussions of immigration control: 'It is the presence of Black people which is causing racism.' Though this assumption was discredited by the mid-1970s, when two out of every five immigrants were born in Britain, yet it continued to be employed, adding to the Black community's frustration and anguish at the fact that their voice was not heard in the public forums of the country, and specifically in the broadcast media.

The Black community branches out

Against this background a vibrant and powerful cultural movement was growing within the Black community, gradually attaining a very distinct Black British flavour. This was evident in the theatre with the creation of Temba Theatre Company, the Black Theatre Co-op and Tara Arts. Equally significantly, the annual Notting Hill Carnival was rapidly becoming Europe's largest festival. Important visual artists too were gaining recognition from major art galleries and institutions, fostered by the Black community's openness to art following the public debate generated by the publication of *The Arts Britain Ignores* report by Naseem Khan in 1976. A more important factor was an increasing tendency of Black artists to organize independently, convinced that it was the most effective way of gaining recognition and reaching their full potential. However, the cultural flowering of these artists in their art forms was not matched by the work of film-makers, if only because of the nature of the medium. The resources required to realize a single feature film were vast.

But this tight financial situation did not deter the likes of Horace Ove. He managed to overcome the obstacles by producing his feature film *Pressure*, the first feature film to come from a Black British film-maker and a major achievement in itself. It was inspired and acted in the main by Black people and considered pioneering also because, for the first time, the medium of film was used to reveal something of the internal drama of the Black condition in the country. The film portrayed the trials and tribulations of a young unemployed youth's attempts to find employment commensurate with his 'O' level secondary-school qualification. When the film was shown at the London Film Festival in 1975, it was greeted with warm, even ecstatic reviews, though it was not without shortcomings. Despite the rather meagre grant from the British Film Institute (BFI), the production still had to rely heavily on technicians donating their services free and on the total commitment of the actors. The excitement that greeted the film at the time was captured in the pages of *Race Today* when it stated: 'He (Ove) has tried to integrate the minutiae of the documentary film with larger ideas and events associated with the feature film. The film's major achievement is that such a coherent, intelligent and disciplined statement about the lives of Blacks should have seen the light of the big screen. Arguably the most important medium for mass culture in our time' (Rugg, 1984).

This film was followed by several other documentaries and art films, including Ove's next film *Reggae* (1978) which centred on an exploration of the roots of this music and its meteoric rise to international significance.

A similar breakthrough occurred with the release of a second feature film, *Burning an Illusion* by Menelik Shabazz, another Black British director. The film confirmed the abundance of talent many believed to exist among the handful of British Black film-makers. He too demonstrated a powerful grasp of the art of film-making. The plot basically was a 'boy meets girl' story but comprised a heady mixture of elements including race, sex and class. All were intertwined in a beautiful drama and were carried off with slick cinematography and able performances. In its own way it shattered the ingrained dramatic formulae that always saw Black people as victims of one thing or another.

The vibrant eighties

As indicated above, the real explosion in Black film-making still lay ahead with, in the 1980s, the rise of the Black workshop movement. The 1980s were a time of ferment with a developing aesthetic and improved prospects for many who were now knocking on the doors of broadcasting institutions for opportunities and resources to apply their talent. A combination of factors, many of them quite fortuitous, triggered this excitingly new and independent production activity. Above all it was due to the creation of the Channel Four TV service and the original dimension in television programming it was charged to introduce. Until that time, the three broadcasters, BBC1, BBC2 and ITV, following the rapid decline of British cinema output, had become responsible for much of the production activity in the country. However, they seldom commissioned work outside their structures and, as a result, Britain had no independent production activity to speak of, save for the small independents doing mainly commissioned work and documentaries, but having only loose informal links with television. And there was of course the art sector, that modest network of a mere handful of individuals, workshops and collectives which started in the 1960s. These enjoyed a relationship with, and were encouraged by, the BFI, the Arts Council of Great Britain (ACGB) and the Regional Arts Associations (RAA, since replaced by the Regional Arts Boards) which funded their art and short film work. Almost all were White artists who were influenced by the counter-culture movement of the time and saw their work as a pursuit of a distinct cultural and aesthetic practice quite different from that operating in the mainstream media. These initiatives provided the model for the independent workshop movement that was being built. Moves had already been made prior to the launch of the new channel to increase the amount of public funding released for film production. The BFI, the ACGB and the RAA, through which all arts funding was routed, were engaged with practitioners throughout the period to secure adequate funding to cover wages in the workshops. But these had reached an impasse by the end of the 1970s. As Ursula Head reported (1991): 'In 1976 discussions between the BFI's regional department and the Arts Association's film officers agreed that it would be desirable to wage film-makers, but for the time being such a provision would be impossible to implement as there was nowhere near enough state money available for the independent sector'.

The Association of Cinematographers (ACCT), together with the Arts Associations and the BFI, had agreed on codes of practice to cover the feature film work which they had started to fund in the mid-1970s. The codes made provision for wages to be paid on a lower scale to enable work to be exhibited or broadcast without obstruction by employees in these organizations. This also enabled these independent workshops to join the union as full members, following the setting up of an ACCT regional branch. It became legitimate following these efforts to view funding of the independent and workshop sector in terms of overheads, wages and a programme of work.

Significantly the case was made and accepted by Channel Four at the time its charter was drawn up, which required it to encourage innovation and experiment in the form and content of its programming. This also encouraged the new channel to look at independents, and the workshop sector, where traditionally experiment and innovation had been the dominant cultural practice.

The workshops declaration

In 1982, the year Channel Four was set up, the Workshops Declaration was promulgated setting out the structure and the terms and conditions of employment in the franchized workshops. It enabled production-based groups to set up a non-profit distributing workshop under workers' control. It had the right to retain copyright and all rights of exploitation of its work, though such workshops were not restricted solely to production. The declaration deemed that a significant proportion of their output must not involve work customarily undertaken under full union agreement. The most important and encouraging achievement of the channel, however, is that it provided 'a means by which television money (not just Channel Four's) not already committed to specific editorial commissions could enter the independent sector' (Head, 1991, p. 12).

Franchized workshops were now able to receive a mixture of funding from television, art funding bodies and local authorities. In return for its financial support, it was agreed that Channel Four would receive at least fifty-two minutes of programming material for each year that a workshop was funded. This agreement, by and large, enabled a wide network of organizations to receive an adequate level of funding without crippling the art funding bodies.

Another element of particular importance for Black workshops was the fact that the impact of the 1981 inner-city uprisings was altering the terms of public policy debates and the need to target resources to address racial disadvantage. Local authorities such as the Greater London Council (GLC), being the strategic authority for the capital, embraced the *Scarman Report* (1982) in deciding to allocate their resources and grants to art organizations. This was soon followed by the Arts Council's Ethnic Minorities Action Plan which posited a new orientation in the leading public art-funding body's policy towards Black arts organizations by increasing levels of support. Six Black film and video workshops were set up on the strength of the Workshop Declaration. They included Ceddo Film and Video Workshop, 1981; Black Audio/Film Collective, 1983; Macro Films, 1983; Sankofa, 1984.

The new Channel throughout its first years encouraged new efforts, taking its responsibilities in bringing new voices to the screen and catering for tastes and needs not served by other Channels. It appointed the first commissioning editor for multi-cultural programming in British TV with a specific brief to bring to the screen work about, or by, Black people (the definition of multi-cultural here includes other minorities in addition to Black ones). Under the first editor and up to the present time, a stream of regular features and current affairs programmes aimed at African, Afro-Caribbean and Asian viewers continue to be broadcast, being supplemented by regular situation comedy series and dramas. Many of these have originated in the corporate production sector. It is interesting to note that many Black producers who were already working in the mainstream before the setting-up of the workshop movement remained there and viewed with suspicion entry into the workshop sector. The work commissioned by the multicultural department came either from those working for large employers or from those in certain production companies, many of which were set up to take on commissions. It was considered the correct course to fight for employment in the mainstream. Many continued to view with suspicion those who opted for the workshop sector. They believed it would 'result in the double marginalization of Black media workers' (Head, 1991, p. 23).

Black films come to stay

The level of output and quality of film-making that came out of the workshop sector completely confounded any suspicions and proved that their achievement was of a completely different order to that of the steady and solid work of those producing in the mainstream. Objectively speaking the two new sources of Black production acted as tributaries that made a unified flow, brimming with plurality and diversity of expression. For the first time in its twenty-five year history, Black film-making in Britain had established an indelible presence within the cultural and artistic life of the country. In the short period from the birth of the Channel and the end of the decade, a body of work had been done that was of sufficient breadth and depth to make it possible to speak of a distinct Black British cinema.

The first feature film to emerge from the workshop sector was *Majdar* (1984), directed by Ahmed Jamal, which shattered the accepted myths of Asian women as placid and silently suffering subjects of tradition. Its central character, Fauzia, is following her journey of emotional growth which takes her beyond the usual social, cultural and religious barriers. Like others that followed, this film registered a shift in the way the experiences of Black people are comprehended and how they are portrayed.

There were real innovative and equally bold statements in the area of documentaries where Black film-makers have always been prodigious, and where traditionally they favour working. The workshop sector afforded particular freedom to work away from the prying eyes of bureaucrats and outside the political control of editors. These films spanned a limited area of concerns but managed real strides in putting across new passions welling up inside the community. A film like *The People's Account*, directed by Glen Masokoane, tells the story of the uprisings in 1985, mainly in Tottenham, through interviews with Black people living on the estate. It was withheld from transmission on the ground that it breached the IBA code in its lack of balance and unsubstantiated claims against the police. In it, the film-makers challenge the accepted rules and the official version of events, extending the allowable limits governing much of the reporting of Black issues on TV. Jim Pines noted the kind of dilemma these producers have to face: 'The general problem therefore seems to turn on the whole question of official discourse regarding Black-related situations, and the struggle among Black independent practitioners to somewhat subvert these discourses while at the same time seeking relatively unimpeded access to the main exhibition and broadcast outlets.'

Breaking these boundaries has been the most enduring aspect of the work of these independent workshops. A good example is the award-winning work of the Black Audio Film Collective's *Handworth Songs* (1987) which won seven international awards including the BFI Grierson Award. It too takes the theme of the 1985 uprisings and attempts to put them in a different, alternative frame. Its meaning derives from its juxtaposition of archive material to create a new and poetic rendition of image and words in a visual essay, a salvo in 'a media war of meaning' which raged around the events. 'There are no stories in the riots, only the ghosts of other stories', commented a Black audio brochure.

Channel Four's contribution

Channel Four became a major funder of the workshops sector. Of twenty-three in 1989, ten were funded by Channel Four. Channel Four in association with the independent workshop sector generated a remarkable growth in film and video production, and was effective in enhancing a production culture at the grass-roots level. Such a development was not consistent with the politics of Thatcherism. Within two years of the Declaration it was becoming clear that the abolition of the Metropolitan Authorities, including the Greater London Council (GLC), by the Thatcher Government, would lead to the crumbling of one of the pillars of this fragile funding arrangement. And when it came, the abolition wreaked havoc with the workshops operating in London at the time. In all, Channel Four funded fifteen franchized and non-franchized workshops including those of Ceddo, Retake and Sankofa, while the GLC, with its policy of extending 'equal opportunities' to minority groups, had benefited Black workshops in an unprecedented way. The knock-on effect of abolition was felt all the more sharply because of the government's slowly tightening grip on public expenditure, whether directly or through its decreasing allocations to the Local Authorities' Support Grant. As a consequence, art and leisure activities suffered very badly.

During the first six years of the workshops, the BFI regional fund provided £230,000 for direct funding to the workshops, but this was gradually reduced, particularly following its change of policy towards the workshops in 1989. The workshops received £110,000 in 1989, increasing to £151,000 in 1991/92. The funding crisis, triggered by the Conservative Government, put a lot of pressure on the funding bodies to re-examine their funding relationship with the workshop sector, and none more than Channel Four which for a time continued to subsidize but gradually pulled back, not least because it saw itself as a partner in an enterprise rather than as the sole funder, and was now gradually becoming, to its great alarm, the dominant partner. There were probably other reasons why Channel Four wanted to re-evaluate its relationship with the workshop sector, not least because of the shape of the television industry emerging in the 1990s with the publication of the White Paper on Government Broadcasting, and the opening of all aspects of television production to competition and market forces. In future the only criterion that would matter with quality coming second was audience share and advertising revenue. Cost-conscious and product-led policies were going to be the strategic consideration of all broadcasters; Channel Four, with its clear remit to meet audience programming needs not met by other broadcasters, is no exception. Clearly, therefore, it must seek to influence the development of the workshops in a direction acceptable to it.

Alan Fountain, Commissioning Editor for Independent Film and Video at

Channel Four, and incidentally a prime mover of the original Workshop Declaration, wrote a paper entitled *Workshops in the Nineties* in which he expounds the view that the Channel will aim for a specific product when considering funding a workshop. The sticking-point it seems was that it did not feel responsible for undertaking funding over the wide range of non-production activities which were intrinsic to the workshop ethos. In theory, of course, it accepted these activities as essentially part of the integrated practice that it regarded as the seed-bed for innovation and creativity while, in reality, pressure was being exerted on workshops 'to deliver made-for-television products'.

To undermine integrated practice is to question the basis of the workshops and the non-commercial nature of the organization. The new policy does so in two ways. *Television with a difference*, the new scheme to which workshops are invited to apply, (i) contracts applicants for a minimum of one year, instead of three years as was previously the case, with no automatic renewals, and (ii) proposes that the scheme be open to applicants from outside the sector. Since Channel Four has to meet its remit, the workshops, Alan Fountain believes, have become staid, comfortable and devoid of ideas because of long-term funding. It is clear that it is abandoning its all-embracing commitment to the workshop sector, along with the original cultural aim. This policy also finds echoes in the policy statement made by the BFI at the same time as Channel Four's *Workshops in the Nineties* was published.

To sum up

The creative and entrepreneurial seed-bed at the heart of the workshop sector has been placed in jeopardy by the simplicities of a policy determined by economic realism in the context of an industry principally determined by market forces. For the independent Black film and video sector, this has meant a severe brake on its ability to consolidate the advances of the workshop movement. It has exposed Black professionals to the harsh competitiveness of the extensive casualization of labour. And this in the context of an industry where many new independent production companies are in fact cloned from teams that have migrated from the BBC and Independent Television channels, under the pressure of deregulation. They of course have the advantage of having their networks intact within mainstream television.

While within the broadcasting industries there have been positive developments which attempt to address the employment of Black persons – the BBC's Equal Opportunities programme is such an instance in the context of a contracting workforce and a slump in staff turnover – these initiatives can only begin to scratch at the surface of a problem born of four decades of complacent neglect. An independent Black film and video sector therefore remains equally vital to nurturing a distinctive cultural-political agenda and aesthetic as to ensuring the continuity of training opportunities for Black persons in Britain.

References

Cohen, P. & Gardner, C. (1982): *It ain't half racist mum: Fighting racism in the media.* London, Comedia.

Dyson, K. & Humphreys, P. (1985): The new media in Britain and in France – two versions of heroic muddle, *Rundfunk und Fernsehen*, No. 33, (3–4), pp. 362–379.

Hartman, P. & Husband, C. (1974): *Racism and the Mass Media.* London, Davis-Poynter.

Head, U. (1991): *The History of the Workshop Movement from the Nineteen Sixties.* Monograph.

H.M.S.O. (1988): *Broadcasting in the '90s* (White Paper).

Husband, C. (1987): *'Race' in Britain: Continuity and Change.* London, Hutchinson.

Husband, C. & Chouhan, J.M. (1985): Local radio in the Communication of Ethnic Minorities in Britain. In: T.A. van Dijk (ed.). *Discourse and Communication.* Berlin, Walter de Gruyter.

Khan, N. (1976): *The Arts Britain Ignores: the Arts of Ethnic Minorities in Britain.* London, Community Relations Commission, p. 15.

Levitas, R. (1986): *The Ideology of the New Right.* London, Polity Press.

Local Radio Workshop (1983): *Nothing Local about It: London's Local Radio.* London, Comedia.

Murray, N. (1986): Anti-racists and other demons: the press and ideology in Thatcher's Britain. In: *Race and Class*, Vol.XXVII, No. 3, Winter.

Odusina, J. (1986): Black arts, struggling to be seen and heard. In: K. Owusu, op. cit.

Owusu, K. (1986): *The Struggle for Black Arts in Britain.* London, Comedia.

Phillips-Eteng, E. (1988): *Black British Consumer Markets.* London, The Planner's Guide.

Pines, J. (1988): Black independent film in Britain. In: J. Twitchin, op. cit.

Pines, J. (1988): *Introduction to the Black Workshops.* London, British Film Institute.

Rugg, A. (1984): *Brickbats and Bouquets.* London, Race Today Publications: 17.

Searle, C. (1987): 'Your daily dose: racism and the *Sun*'. In: *Race and Class.* Vol. XXIX, No. 1, Summer.

Seidel, J. (1986): Culture, Nation and 'Race' in the British and French New Right. In: R. Levitas, op. cit.

Troyna, B. (1987): Reporting racism: The 'British way of life' observed. In: C. Husband, op. cit.

Twitchin, J. (1988): *The Black and White Media Book.* Stoke on Trent, Trentham Books.

van Dijk, T.A. (1991): *Racism and the Press.* London, Routledge.

Conclusion

Charles Husband

The chapters of this book have illustrated the vitality of ethnic minority communities in generating ethnic minority media production, in participating creatively within mainstream media and in exploring institutional frameworks that will sustain the viability of their contribution to national and international mass communication. The same chapters have also indicated the very many factors which inhibit, and indeed resist, the democratization of the mass media in order to reflect more accurately, and service more appropriately, multi-ethnic societies. The relation of communication systems to the full expression of citizenship within contemporary nation-states, as sketched by Murdock in our introductory chapter, seems on the basis of the case material provided here to be far removed from the ideal he defines.

Clearly the political entity of the nation-state is not ethnically neutral, and the de facto reality of its multi-ethnic citizenry sits uneasily with the normative ethnic agenda dictated through the hegemonic activities of the dominant ethnic grouping. Where ethnicity is entwined in the politics of nationalism, then a free democratic interplay of cultures within an ethnically pluralist mass media becomes even less likely. The relatively recent immigration of ethnic minorities, and their settlement in the countries represented in this book, has come at a time of major change in the structure of international capital, with attended social change, and upheaval, in each country. Ethnic minority communities and the context for ethnic minority media production cannot be seen within any narrow national agenda.

Ethnic minority communities are transnational in their history and contemporary identities, and the nation-state is not a terrain within which their interests may be contained. One of the major functions of ethnic minority media is to express the unique historical experience of ethnic communities and articulate its relation to their current situation. While there is a shared experience of migration and settlement that provides a basis for collaboration and mutual support between ethnic minority communities, as illustrated by Radio Immigranten and the Black British film movement, distinct ethnicity will not be reduced to 'migrant' status. Thus ethnic minority media production must of necessity reflect the specific experience, politics and aesthetics of distinct ethnic communities. And the demography of ethnic minority settlement may mean that 'local media' (radio, press and cable) can best serve these specific needs, which is not to say that the mainstream media can accordingly be absolved of responsibility to address them, as Bovenkerk-Teerink suggests the Dutch Government wishes to do. The specific concerns of ethnic minority communities are not detached from the universal existential agendas of all citizens. And in multi-ethnic societies, recognizing difference and considering its implications within a democratic society ought to be a legitimate concern of mainstream media.

Of course, as the examples in this work illustrate, the structural location of ethnic minorities within Western democracies is itself a reflection of their marginal status as citizens of the societies in which they dwell. Consequently the political agendas and personal experiences of ethnic minority communities are hardly likely to be compatible with nurturing the positive self-regard of the dominant ethnic groups. State media policies tend towards the promotion of a national consensus, whereas a democratic and pluralist media would generate a partisan and contentious reality. Whereas the state seeks to promote similarity and consensus, multi-ethnic democracy must provide a forum for difference and dialogue. As Hussein points out in relation to the British situation, ethnic minority producers aspire to engage with popular cultures rather than with an élite 'high culture' or ersatz 'national culture'. Popular cultures are engaged in a struggle with the values, imagery and institutional practices of the dominant culture, and consequently consensus is not an available option; nor, for that matter, are disagreement and dialogue anti-democratic. As the material in this book indicates, there is also a need to articulate the difference and disagreement in and between ethnic minority communities.

Ethnic minority policy within a state very clearly impacts upon the ethnic minority media environment. The cases of Australia, the Netherlands and Norway, for example, demonstrate that the state may intervene to provide a financial basis in order to stimulate an ethnic minority media sector. The parsimony and constraints attached to these activities are themselves indicative of the inherent link between ethnic minority policies and communication policies. The capital and operational costs of media production have emerged as a major problem in attempting to establish an ethnic minority media sector. Consequently state subsidy remains as one obvious necessary response to the reality of recent settlement, small target audiences and the high start-up costs that face ethnic minority media. A close reading of the examples above would, however, lead to scepticism regarding the political pragmatism informing such state support, and the constraints on autonomy that attach to it.

It is equally clear from the case-studies that the practice and values of public service broadcasting are experiencing a damaging assault, often expressed politically, but focused through the economic consequences of media deregulation. While the introductory chapter questioned the extent of democratic pluralism afforded by public service broadcasting (PSB), there has been frequent lamenting at the social implications of the loss of the public service broadcasting tradition and its usurpation by the selfish profit motive of Mammon. With regard to ethnic minority communities the track record of broadcast media carrying the PSB imprimatur has been unimpressive; and the public service tradition represents more of a promise unfulfilled than a valued service newly threatened or else lost. The values espoused within the public service tradition do, however, continue to be relevant to the special needs and rights of ethnic minority media audiences. Nor, it should be said, are commercial media and the profit motive inimical to ethnic minority media. With audience fragmentation and the identification of appropriate media, commercial media interests can well lead to the identification, and servicing, of ethnic minority audiences. Some doubt remains, however, as to the range and quality of media that would be available were purely commercial considerations the sole criteria. For example, 'popular culture' as conveyed by ethnic minority radio tends too easily to be reduced to popular music.

Whether in public or commercial media the situation of the ethnic minority professional remains a problematic one. The preceding chapters highlight the dangers of marginalization through ethnic specialization, and the institutional racism which disadvantages the ethnic minority employee. As long as 'being professional' means shedding one's ethnic identity, then equal opportunities recruitment policies will remain inconsequential. Such policies do not of themselves guarantee that media institutions reflect non-racist, multi-ethnic pluralism in their products. As the present texts show, mere visibility of ethnic minority personnel is no guarantee of a more fundamental challenge to ethnic hegemony within a media institution. To repeat what I said in my introductory chapter, the removal of discrimination from the mainstream media and a readily permeable interface between mainstream and ethnic minority media are basic requirements of the media industries in multi-ethnic societies.

The present study has its origins in the programme of work supported by UNESCO which explores the role of information and other media in securing the human rights of ethnic minorities. While the book does not contain an analysis of the role of international declarations and agreements relating to the communication rights of ethnic minorities, the evidence presented here would appear to suggest that national governments and media institutions pay scant regard to these. However, their importance should not be underestimated. They act as a benchmark for monitoring progress and provide a specific point of leverage for those promoting change. Their political relevance is unobtrusively suggested by the extent to which they are deliberately neglected. The defence of a myopic definition of national identity and an unchanged, and unchangeable, conception of the order of things are not compatible with recognizing the ethnic diversity of our nations and the human and communication rights of ethnic minority persons. The struggle to achieve equity for their communities in the media industries is an assertion of the communication rights of all persons. Media democratization cannot be pursued within a media apartheid: our aim should be a richer vision for all.

Media titles available from John Libbey

Acamedia Research Monographs

Satellite Television in Western Europe (revised edition 1992)
Richard Collins
Hardback ISBN 0 86196 203 6

Beyond the Berne Convention
Copyright, Broadcasting and the Single European Market
Vincent Porter
Hardback ISBN 0 86196 267 2

Nuclear Reactions: A Study in Public Issue Television
John Corner, Kay Richardson and Natalie Fenton
Hardback ISBN 0 86196 251 6

Transnationalization of Television in Western Europe
Preben Sepstrup
Hardback ISBN 0 86196 280 X

The People's Voice: Local Radio and Television in Europe
Nick Jankowski, Ole Prehn and James Stappers
Hardback ISBN 0 86196 322 9

Television and the Gulf War
David E. Morrison
Hardback ISBN 0 86196 341 5

Contra-Flow in Global News
Oliver Boyd Barrett and Daya Kishan Thussu
Hardback ISBN 0 86196 344 X

CNN World Report: Ted Turner's International News Coup
Don M. Flournoy
Hardback ISBN 0 86196 359 8

Small Nations: Big Neighbour
Roger de la Garde, William Gilsdorf and Ilja Wechselmann
Hardback ISBN 0 86196 343 1

BBC Annual Research Reviews

Annual Review of BBC Broadcasting Research: No XV - 1989
Paperback ISBN 0 86196 209 5

Annual Review of BBC Broadcasting Research: No XVI - 1990
Paperback ISBN 0 86196 265 6

Annual Review of BBC Broadcasting Research: No XVII - 1991
Paperback ISBN 0 86196 319 9

Annual Review of BBC Broadcasting Research: No XVIII - 1992
Paperback ISBN 0 86196 368 7
Peter Menneer (ed)

European Media Research Series

The New Television in Europe
Edited by Alessandro Silj
Hardback ISBN 0 86196 361 X

Media Industry in Europe
Edited by Antonio Pilati
Paperback ISBN 0 86196 398 9

Media titles available from John Libbey

Broadcasting and Audio-visual Policy in the European Single Market
Richard Collins
Hardback ISBN 0 86196 405 5

Aid for Cinematographic and Audio-visual Production In Europe
(published for the Council of Europe)
Jean-Noël Dibie
Hardback ISBN 0 86196 397 0

BBC World Service

Global Audiences: Research for Worldwide Broadcasting 1993
Edited by Graham Mytton
Paperback ISBN 0 86196 400 4

Broadcasting Standards Council Publications

A Measure of Uncertainty: The Effects of the Mass Media
Guy Cumberbatch and Dennis Howitt
Hardback ISBN 0 86196 231 1

Violence in Television Fiction: Public Opinion and Broadcasting Standards
David Docherty
Paperback ISBN 0 86196 284 2

Survivors and the Media
Ann Shearer
Paperback ISBN 0 86196 332 6

Taste and Decency in Broadcasting
Andrea Millwood Hargrave
Paperback ISBN 0 86196 331 8

A Matter of Manners? – The Limits of Broadcast Language
Edited by Andrea Millwood Hargrave
Paperback ISBN 0 86196 337 7

Sex and Sexuality in Broadcasting
Andrea Millwood Hargrave
Paperback ISBN 0 86196 393 8

Violence in Factual Television
Andrea Millwood Hargrave
Paperback ISBN 0 86196 441 1

Broadcasting Research Unit Monographs

Invisible Citizens:
British Public Opinion and the Future of Broadcasting
David E. Morrison
Paperback ISBN 0 86196 111 0

Keeping Faith? Channel Four and its Audience
David Docherty, David E. Morrison and Michael Tracey
Paperback ISBN 0 86196 158 7

Quality in Television –
Programmes, Programme-makers, Systems
Richard Hoggart (ed)
Paperback ISBN 0 86196 237 0

Media titles available from John Libbey

School Television in Use
Diana Moses and Paul Croll
Paperback ISBN 0 86196 308 3

UNESCO Publications

Video World-Wide: An International Study
Manuel Alvarado (ed)
Paperback ISBN 0 86196 143 9

University of Manchester Broadcasting Symposium

And Now for the BBC ...
Proceedings of the 22nd Symposium 1991
Nod Miller and Rod Allen (eds)
Paperback ISBN 0 86196 318 0

It's Live – But Is It Real?
Proceedings of the 23rd Symposium 1992
Nod Miller and Rod Allen (eds)
Paperback ISBN 0 86196 370 9

Published in association with The Arts Council

Picture This: Media Representations of Visual Art and Artists
Philip Hayward (ed)
Paperback ISBN 0 86196 126 9

Culture, Technology and Creativity
Philip Hayward (ed)
Paperback ISBN 0 86196 266 4

Parallel Lines: Media Representations of Dance
Stephanie Jordan & Dave Allen (eds)
Paperback ISBN 0 86196 371 7

Arts TV: A History of British Arts Television
John A Walker
Paperback ISBN 0 86196 435 7

ITC Television Research Monographs

Television in Schools
Robin Moss, Christopher Jones and Barrie Gunter
Hardback ISBN 0 86196 314 8

Television: The Public's View
Barrie Gunter and Carmel McLaughlin
Hardback ISBN 0 86196 348 2

The Reactive Viewer
Barrie Gunter and Mallory Wober
Hardback ISBN 0 86196 358 X

Television: The Public's View 1992
Barrie Gunter and Paul Winstone
Hardback ISBN 0 86196 399 7

Seeing is Believing: Religion and Television in the 1990s
Barrie Gunter and Rachel Viney
Hardback ISBN 0 86196 442 X

Media titles available from John Libbey

IBA Television Research Monographs

Teachers and Television:
A History of the IBA's Educational Fellowship Scheme
Josephine Langham
Hardback ISBN 0 86196 264 8

Godwatching: Viewers, Religion and Television
Michael Svennevig, Ian Haldane, Sharon Spiers and Barrie Gunter
Hardback ISBN 0 86196 198 6
Paperback ISBN 0 86196 199 4

Violence on Television: What the Viewers Think
Barrie Gunter and Mallory Wober
Hardback ISBN 0 86196 171 4
Paperback ISBN 0 86196 172 2

Home Video and the Changing Nature of Television Audience
Mark Levy and Barrie Gunter
Hardback ISBN 0 86196 175 7
Paperback ISBN 0 86196 188 9

Patterns of Teletext Use in the UK
Bradley S. Greenberg and Carolyn A. Lin
Hardback ISBN 0 86196 174 9
Paperback ISBN 0 86196 187 0

Attitudes to Broadcasting Over the Years
Barrie Gunter and Michael Svennevig
Hardback ISBN 0 86196 173 0
Paperback ISBN 0 86196 184 6

Television and Sex Role Stereotyping
Barrie Gunter
Hardback ISBN 0 86196 095 5
Paperback ISBN 0 86196 098 X

Television and the Fear of Crime
Barrie Gunter
Hardback ISBN 0 86196 118 8
Paperback ISBN 0 86196 119 6

Behind and in Front of the Screen – Television's Involvement with Family Life
Barrie Gunter and Michael Svennevig
Hardback ISBN 0 86196 123 4
Paperback ISBN 0 86196 124 2

Institute of Local Television

Citizen Television: A Local Dimension to Public Service Broadcasting
Dave Rushton (ed)
Hardback ISBN 0 86196 433 0

Reporters Sans Frontières

1993 Report
Freedom of the Press Throughout the World
Paperback ISBN 0 86196 403 9